D0451007

C# 8.0 Pocket Reference
*Instant Help for C# 8.0
Programmers*

Joseph Albahari and Ben Albahari

Beijing · Boston · Farnham · Sebastopol · Tokyo

C# 8.0 Pocket Reference

by Joseph Albahari and Ben Albahari

Copyright © 2020 Joseph Albahari and Ben Albahari. All rights reserved.

Printed in Canada.

Published by O'Reilly Media, Inc., 1005 Gravenstein Highway North, Sebastopol, CA 95472.

O'Reilly books may be purchased for educational, business, or sales promotional use. Online editions are also available for most titles (*http://oreilly.com*). For more information, contact our corporate/institutional sales department: 800-998-9938 or *corporate@oreilly.com*.

Editors: Rachel Roumeliotis and Corbin Collins
Production Editor: Kristen Brown
Copyeditor: Octal Publishing, LLC
Proofreader: Christina Edwards
Indexer: Judy McConville
Interior Designer: David Futato
Cover Designer: Karen Montgomery
Illustrator: Rebecca Demarest

November 2019:   First Edition

Revision History for the First Edition
    2019-10-24:   First Release

See *https://oreil.ly/c8pr_errata* for release details.

978-1-492-05121-3

[MBP]

Table of Contents

C# 8.0 Pocket Reference

C# is a general-purpose, type-safe, object-oriented programming language, the goal of which is programmer productivity. To this end, the language balances simplicity, expressiveness, and performance. C# 8 is designed to work the Microsoft *.NET Core 3* runtime, and .NET Standard 2.1 (whereas C# 7 was designed to work with the Microsoft *.NET Framework* 4.6/4.7/4.8 as well as .NET Core 2.x and .NET Standard 2.0).

NOTE

The programs and code snippets in this book mirror those in Chapters 2 through 4 of *C# 8.0 in a Nutshell* and are all available as interactive samples in LINQPad (*http://www.linqpad.net/*). Working through these samples in conjunction with the book accelerates learning in that you can edit the samples and instantly see the results without needing to set up projects and solutions in Visual Studio.

To download the samples, click the Samples tab in LINQPad and then click "Download more samples." LINQPad is free—go to *http://www.linqpad.net*.

A First C# Program

Here is a program that multiplies 12 by 30 and prints the result, 360, to the screen. The double forward slash indicates that the remainder of a line is a *comment*:

```
using System;              // Importing namespace

class Test                 // Class declaration
{
  static void Main()       // Method declaration
  {
    int x = 12 * 30;       // Statement 1
    Console.WriteLine (x); // Statement 2
  }                        // End of method
}                          // End of class
```

At the heart of this program lie two *statements*. Statements in C# execute sequentially and are terminated by a semicolon. The first statement computes the *expression* 12 * 30 and stores the result in a *local variable*, named x, which is an integer type. The second statement calls the Console class's WriteLine *method*, to print the variable x to a text window on the screen.

A *method* performs an action in a series of statements, called a *statement block*—a pair of braces containing zero or more statements. We defined a single method named Main.

Writing higher-level functions that call upon lower-level functions simplifies a program. We can *refactor* our program with a reusable method that multiplies an integer by 12, as follows:

```
using System;

class Test
{
  static void Main()
  {
    Console.WriteLine (FeetToInches (30));   // 360
    Console.WriteLine (FeetToInches (100));  // 1200
  }

  static int FeetToInches (int feet)
  {
```

```
        int inches = feet * 12;
        return inches;
    }
}
```

A return types method can receive *input* data from the caller by specifying *parameters*, and *output* data back to the caller by specifying a *return type*. In the preceding example, we defined a method called `FeetToInches` that has a parameter for inputting feet, and a return type for outputting inches, both of type `int` (integer).

The *literals* `30` and `100` are the *arguments* passed to the `Feet ToInches` method. The `Main` method in our example has empty parentheses because it has no parameters and is `void` because it doesn't return any value to its caller. C# recognizes a method called `Main` as signaling the default entry point of execution. The `Main` method can optionally return an integer (rather than `void`) in order to return a value to the execution environment. The `Main` method can also optionally accept an array of strings as a parameter (that will be populated with any arguments passed to the executable). For example:

```
static int Main (string[] args) {...}
```

NOTE

An array (such as `string[]`) represents a fixed number of elements of a particular type (see "Arrays" on page 31).

Methods are one of several kinds of functions in C#. Another kind of function we used was the * *operator*, which performs multiplication. There are also *constructors*, *properties*, *events*, *indexers*, and *finalizers*.

In our example, the two methods are grouped into a class. A *class* groups function members and data members to form an object-oriented building block. The `Console` class groups members that handle command-line input/output functionality, such as the WriteLine method. Our Test class groups two methods—the Main method and the FeetToInches method. A class is a kind of *type*, which we examine later in "Type Basics" on page 8.

At the outermost level of a program, types are organized into *namespaces*. The using directive makes the System namespace available to our application to use the Console class. We could define all of our classes within the TestPrograms namespace, as follows:

```
using System;

namespace TestPrograms
{
    class Test  {...}
    class Test2 {...}
}
```

The .NET Core libraries are organized into nested namespaces. For example, this is the namespace that contains types for handling text:

```
using System.Text;
```

The using directive is there for convenience; you can also refer to a type by its fully qualified name, which is the type name prefixed with its namespace, such as System.Text.String Builder.

Compilation

The C# compiler compiles source code, specified as a set of files with the *.cs* extension, into an *assembly*, which is the unit of packaging and deployment in .NET. An assembly can be either an *application* or a *library*, the difference being that an application has an entry point ("Main" method), whereas a library does not. The purpose of a library is to be called upon (*referenced*) by an application or other libraries. The .NET Core runtime (and the .NET Framework) comprise a set of libraries.

To invoke the compiler, you can either use an integrated development environment (IDE) such as Visual Studio or Visual Studio Code, or call it manually from the command line. To manually compile a console application with .NET Core, first download the .NET Core SDK, and then create a new project, as follows:

```
dotnet new console -o MyFirstProgram
cd MyFirstProgram
```

This creates a folder called MyFirstProgram, which contains a C# file called *Program.cs*, which you can then edit. To invoke the compiler, call dotnet build (or dotnet run, which will compile and then run the program). The output will be written to a subdirectory under *bin\debug*, which will include *MyFirstProgram.dll* (the output assembly) as well as *MyFirstProgram.exe* (which runs the compiled program directly).

Syntax

C# syntax is inspired by C and C++ syntax. In this section, we describe C#'s elements of syntax, using the following program:

```
using System;

class Test
{
  static void Main()
  {
    int x = 12 * 30;
    Console.WriteLine (x);
  }
}
```

Identifiers and Keywords

Identifiers are names that programmers choose for their classes, methods, variables, and so on. These are the identifiers in our example program, in the order in which they appear:

```
System   Test   Main   x   Console   WriteLine
```

An identifier must be a whole word, essentially made up of Unicode characters starting with a letter or underscore. C# identifiers are case-sensitive. By convention, parameters, local variables, and private fields should be in camel case (e.g., myVariable), and all other identifiers should be in Pascal case (e.g., MyMethod).

Keywords are names that mean something special to the compiler. These are the keywords in our example program:

```
using   class   static   void   int
```

Most keywords are *reserved*, which means that you can't use them as identifiers. Here is the full list of C# reserved keywords:

abstract	enum	long	stackalloc
as	event	namespace	static
base	explicit	new	string
bool	extern	null	struct
break	false	object	switch
byte	finally	operator	this
case	fixed	out	throw
catch	float	override	true
char	for	params	try
checked	foreach	private	typeof
class	goto	protected	uint
const	if	public	ulong
continue	implicit	readonly	unchecked
decimal	in	ref	unsafe
default	int	return	ushort
delegate	interface	sbyte	using
do	internal	sealed	virtual
double	is	short	void
else	lock	sizeof	while

Avoiding conflicts

If you really want to use an identifier that clashes with a reserved keyword, you can do so by qualifying it with the @ prefix. For instance:

```
class class {...}      // Illegal
class @class {...}     // Legal
```

The @ symbol doesn't form part of the identifier itself. So @myVariable is the same as myVariable.

Contextual keywords

Some keywords are *contextual*, meaning they can also be used as identifiers—without an @ symbol. The contextual keywords are as follows:

add	dynamic	join	select
alias	equals	let	set
ascending	from	nameof	value
async	get	on	var
await	global	orderby	when
by	group	partial	where
descending	into	remove	yield

With contextual keywords, ambiguity cannot arise within the context in which they are used.

Literals, Punctuators, and Operators

Literals are primitive pieces of data lexically embedded into the program. The literals in our example program are 12 and 30. *Punctuators* help demarcate the structure of the program. The punctuators in our program are {, }, and ;.

The braces group multiple statements into a *statement block*. The semicolon terminates a (nonblock) statement. Statements can wrap multiple lines:

```
Console.WriteLine
    (1 + 2 + 3 + 4 + 5 + 6 + 7 + 8 + 9 + 10);
```

An *operator* transforms and combines expressions. Most operators in C# are denoted with a symbol, such as the multiplication operator, *. Here are the operators in our program:

```
.  ()   *   =
```

A period denotes a member of something (or a decimal point with numeric literals). The parentheses, in our example, appear where we declare or call a method; empty parentheses mean that the method accepts no arguments. The equals sign performs *assignment* (the double equals, ==, performs equality comparison).

Comments

C# offers two different styles of source code documentation: *single-line comments* and *multiline comments*. A single-line comment begins with a double forward slash and continues until the end of the line. For example:

```
int x = 3;   // Comment about assigning 3 to x
```

A multiline comment begins with /* and ends with */. For example:

```
int x = 3;   /* This is a comment that
                spans two lines */
```

Comments can embed XML documentation tags (see "XML Documentation" on page 222).

Type Basics

A *type* defines the blueprint for a value. In our example, we used two literals of type int with values 12 and 30. We also declared a *variable* of type int whose name was x.

A *variable* denotes a storage location that can contain different values over time. In contrast, a *constant* always represents the same value (more on this later).

All values in C# are an *instance* of a specific type. The meaning of a value, and the set of possible values a variable can have, is determined by its type.

Predefined Type Examples

Predefined types (also called *built-in* types) are types that are specially supported by the compiler. The int type is a predefined type for representing the set of integers that fit into 32 bits of memory, from -2^{31} to $2^{31}-1$. We can perform functions such as arithmetic with instances of the int type as follows:

```
int x = 12 * 30;
```

Another predefined C# type is string. The string type represents a sequence of characters, such as ".NET" or "*http:// oreilly.com*". We can work with strings by calling functions on them, as follows:

```
string message = "Hello world";
string upperMessage = message.ToUpper();
Console.WriteLine (upperMessage);        // HELLO WORLD

int x = 2015;
message = message + x.ToString();
Console.WriteLine (message);             // Hello world2015
```

The predefined bool type has exactly two possible values: true and false. The bool type is commonly used to conditionally branch execution flow with an if statement. For example:

```
bool simpleVar = false;
if (simpleVar)
  Console.WriteLine ("This will not print");

int x = 5000;
bool lessThanAMile = x < 5280;
if (lessThanAMile)
  Console.WriteLine ("This will print");
```

The System namespace in .NET Core contains many important types that are not predefined by C# (e.g., Date Time).

Custom Type Examples

Just as we can build complex functions from simple functions, we can build complex types from primitive types. In this example, we will define a custom type named UnitConverter—a class that serves as a blueprint for unit conversions:

```
using System;

public class UnitConverter
{
  int ratio;                          // Field

  public UnitConverter (int unitRatio)  // Constructor
  {
    ratio = unitRatio;
  }

  public int Convert (int unit)         // Method
  {
    return unit * ratio;
  }
}

class Test
{
  static void Main()
  {
    UnitConverter feetToInches = new UnitConverter(12);
    UnitConverter milesToFeet = new UnitConverter(5280);

    Console.Write (feetToInches.Convert(30));   // 360
    Console.Write (feetToInches.Convert(100));  // 1200
    Console.Write (feetToInches.Convert
                    (milesToFeet.Convert(1)));  // 63360
  }
}
```

Members of a type

A type contains *data members* and *function members*. The data member of UnitConverter is the *field* called ratio. The function members of UnitConverter are the Convert method and the UnitConverter's *constructor*.

Symmetry of predefined types and custom types

A beautiful aspect of C# is that predefined types and custom types have few differences. The predefined int type serves as a blueprint for integers. It holds data—32 bits—and provides function members that use that data, such as ToString. Similarly, our custom UnitConverter type acts as a blueprint for unit conversions. It holds data—the ratio—and provides function members to use that data.

Constructors and instantiation

Data is created by *instantiating* a type. We can instantiate predefined types simply by using a literal such as 12 or "Hello world".

The new operator creates instances of a custom type. We started our Main method by creating two instances of the UnitConverter type. Immediately after the new operator instantiates an object, the object's *constructor* is called to perform initialization. A constructor is defined like a method, except that the method name and return type are reduced to the name of the enclosing type:

```
public UnitConverter (int unitRatio)   // Constructor
{
  ratio = unitRatio;
}
```

Instance versus static members

The data members and function members that operate on the *instance* of the type are called instance members. The UnitConverter's Convert method and the int's ToString method are examples of instance members. By default, members are instance members.

Data members and function members that don't operate on the instance of the type, but rather on the type itself, must be marked as `static`. The `Test.Main` and `Console.WriteLine` methods are static methods. The `Console` class is actually a *static class*, which means *all* of its members are static. You never actually create instances of a `Console`—one console is shared across the entire application.

Let's contrast instance with static members. In the following code, the instance field `Name` pertains to an instance of a particular `Panda`, whereas `Population` pertains to the set of all `Panda` instances:

```
public class Panda
{
  public string Name;            // Instance field
  public static int Population;  // Static field

  public Panda (string n)        // Constructor
  {
    Name = n;                    // Assign instance field
    Population = Population+1;    // Increment static field
  }
}
```

The following code creates two instances of the `Panda`, prints their names, and then prints the total population:

```
Panda p1 = new Panda ("Pan Dee");
Panda p2 = new Panda ("Pan Dah");

Console.WriteLine (p1.Name);      // Pan Dee
Console.WriteLine (p2.Name);      // Pan Dah

Console.WriteLine (Panda.Population);   // 2
```

The public keyword

The `public` keyword exposes members to other classes. In this example, if the `Name` field in `Panda` was not marked as public, it would be private and the `Test` class could not access it.

Marking a member public is how a type communicates: "Here is what I want other types to see—everything else is my own private implementation details." In object-oriented terms, we say that the public members *encapsulate* the private members of the class.

Conversions

C# can convert between instances of compatible types. A conversion always creates a new value from an existing one. Conversions can be either *implicit* or *explicit*: implicit conversions happen automatically, whereas explicit conversions require a *cast*. In the following example, we *implicitly* convert an int to a long type (which has twice the bit-capacity of an int) and *explicitly* cast an int to a short type (which has half the bit-capacity of an int):

```
int x = 12345;       // int is a 32-bit integer
long y = x;          // Implicit conversion to 64-bit int
short z = (short)x;  // Explicit conversion to 16-bit int
```

In general, implicit conversions are allowed when the compiler can guarantee that they will always succeed without loss of information. Otherwise, you must perform an explicit cast to convert between compatible types.

Value Types versus Reference Types

C# types can be divided into *value types* and *reference types*.

Value types comprise most built-in types (specifically, all numeric types, the char type, and the bool type) as well as custom struct and enum types. *Reference types* comprise all class, array, delegate, and interface types.

The fundamental difference between value types and reference types is how they are handled in memory.

Value types

The content of a *value type* variable or constant is simply a value. For example, the content of the built-in value type int is 32 bits of data.

You can define a custom value type with the struct keyword (see Figure 1):

```
public struct Point { public int X, Y; }
```

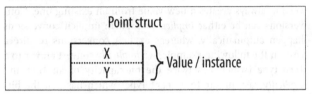

Figure 1. A value type instance in memory

The assignment of a value type instance always *copies* the instance. For example:

```
Point p1 = new Point();
p1.X = 7;

Point p2 = p1;              // Assignment causes copy

Console.WriteLine (p1.X);   // 7
Console.WriteLine (p2.X);   // 7

p1.X = 9;                   // Change p1.X
Console.WriteLine (p1.X);   // 9
Console.WriteLine (p2.X);   // 7
```

Figure 2 shows that p1 and p2 have independent storage.

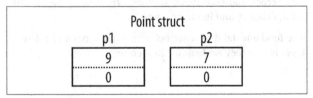

Figure 2. Assignment copies a value type instance

Reference types

A reference type is more complex than a value type, having two parts: an *object* and the *reference* to that object. The content of a reference type variable or constant is a reference to an object that contains the value. Here is the Point type from our previous example rewritten as a class (see Figure 3):

```
public class Point { public int X, Y; }
```

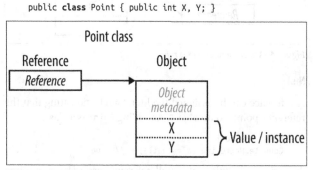

Figure 3. A reference type instance in memory

Assigning a reference type variable copies the reference, not the object instance. This allows multiple variables to refer to the same object—something that's not ordinarily possible with value types. If we repeat the previous example, but with Point now a class, an operation via p1 affects p2:

```
Point p1 = new Point();
p1.X = 7;

Point p2 = p1;              // Copies p1 reference

Console.WriteLine (p1.X);   // 7
Console.WriteLine (p2.X);   // 7

p1.X = 9;                   // Change p1.X
Console.WriteLine (p1.X);   // 9
Console.WriteLine (p2.X);   // 9
```

Figure 4 shows that p1 and p2 are two references that point to the same object.

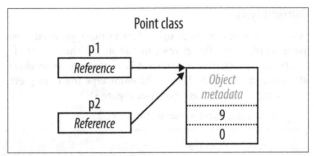

Figure 4. Assignment copies a reference

Null

A reference can be assigned the literal null, indicating that the reference points to no object. Assuming Point is a class:

```
Point p = null;
Console.WriteLine (p == null);   // True
```

Accessing a member of a null reference generates a runtime error:

```
Console.WriteLine (p.X);   // NullReferenceException
```

NOTE

C# 8 introduces a new feature to reduce accidental NullRe
ferenceException errors. For more information, see
"Nullable Reference Types (C# 8)" on page 154.

In contrast, a value type cannot ordinarily have a null value:

```
struct Point {...}
...
Point p = null;  // Compile-time error
int x = null;    // Compile-time error
```

Predefined Type Taxonomy

The predefined types in C# are:

Value types

- Numeric:
    - Signed integer (sbyte, short, int, long)
    - Unsigned integer (byte, ushort, uint, ulong)
    - Real number (float, double, decimal)
- Logical (bool)
- Character (char)

Reference types

- String (string)
- Object (object)

Predefined types in C# alias .NET Core types in the System
namespace. There is only a syntactic difference between these
two statements:

```
int i = 5;
System.Int32 i = 5;
```

The set of predefined *value* types excluding decimal are known
as *primitive types* in the Common Language Runtime (CLR).
Primitive types are so called because they are supported
directly via instructions in compiled code, which usually translates to direct support on the underlying processor.

Numeric Types

C# has the following predefined numeric types:

C# type	System type	Suffix	Size	Range
Integral—signed				
sbyte	SByte		8 bits	-2^7 to 2^7-1
short	Int16		16 bits	-2^{15} to $2^{15}-1$
int	Int32		32 bits	-2^{31} to $2^{31}-1$
long	Int64	L	64 bits	-2^{63} to $2^{63}-1$
Integral—unsigned				
byte	Byte		8 bits	0 to 2^8-1
ushort	UInt16		16 bits	0 to $2^{16}-1$
uint	UInt32	U	32 bits	0 to $2^{32}-1$
ulong	UInt64	UL	64 bits	0 to $2^{64}-1$
Real				
float	Single	F	32 bits	$\pm$ ($\sim10^{-45}$ to 10^{38})
double	Double	D	64 bits	$\pm$ ($\sim10^{-324}$ to 10^{308})
decimal	Decimal	M	128 bits	$\pm$ ($\sim10^{-28}$ to 10^{28})

Of the *integral* types, int and long are first-class citizens and are favored by both C# and the runtime. The other integral types are typically used for interoperability or when space efficiency is paramount.

Of the *real* number types, float and double are called *floating-point types* and are typically used for scientific and graphical calculations. The decimal type is typically used for financial calculations, where base-10-accurate arithmetic and high precision are required. (Technically, decimal is a floating-point type, too, although it's not generally referred to as such.)

Numeric Literals

Integral-typed literals can use decimal or hexadecimal notation; hexadecimal is denoted with the `0x` prefix (e.g., `0x7f` is equivalent to `127`). From C# 7, you can also use the `0b` prefix for binary literals. *Real literals* can use decimal or exponential notation such as `1E06`.

From C# 7, underscores may be inserted within (or before) a numeric literal to improve readability (e.g., `1_000_000`).

Numeric literal type inference

By default, the compiler *infers* a numeric literal to be either `double` or an integral type:

- If the literal contains a decimal point or the exponential symbol (`E`), it is a `double`.
- Otherwise, the literal's type is the first type in this list that can fit the literal's value: `int`, `uint`, `long`, and `ulong`.

For example:

```
Console.Write (        1.0.GetType());  // Double (double)
Console.Write (       1E06.GetType());  // Double (double)
Console.Write (          1.GetType());  // Int32  (int)
Console.Write (0xF0000000.GetType());  // UInt32 (uint)
Console.Write (0x100000000.GetType()); // Int64  (long)
```

Numeric suffixes

The *numeric suffixes* listed in the preceding table explicitly define the type of a literal:

```
decimal d = 3.5M;   // M = decimal (case-insensitive)
```

The suffixes `U` and `L` are rarely necessary, because the `uint`, `long`, and `ulong` types can nearly always be either *inferred* or *implicitly converted* from int:

```
long i = 5;     // Implicit conversion from int to long
```

The D suffix is technically redundant in that all literals with a decimal point are inferred to be double (and you can always add a decimal point to a numeric literal). The F and M suffixes are the most useful and are mandatory when you're specifying fractional float or decimal literals. Without suffixes, the following would not compile, because 4.5 would be inferred to be of type double, which has no implicit conversion to float or decimal:

```
float f = 4.5F;        // Won't compile without suffix
decimal d = -1.23M;    // Won't compile without suffix
```

Numeric Conversions

Integral-to-integral conversions

Integral conversions are *implicit* when the destination type can represent every possible value of the source type. Otherwise, an *explicit* conversion is required. For example:

```
int x = 12345;         // int is a 32-bit integral type
long y = x;            // Implicit conversion to 64-bit int
short z = (short)x;    // Explicit conversion to 16-bit int
```

Real-to-real conversions

A float can be implicitly converted to a double because a double can represent every possible float value. The reverse conversion must be explicit.

Conversions between decimal and other real types must be explicit.

Real-to-integral conversions

Conversions from integral types to real types are implicit, whereas the reverse must be explicit. Converting from a floating-point to an integral type truncates any fractional portion; to perform rounding conversions, use the static System.Convert class.

A caveat is that implicitly converting a large integral type to a floating-point type preserves *magnitude* but might occasionally lose *precision*:

```
int i1 = 100000001;
float f = i1;      // Magnitude preserved, precision lost
int i2 = (int)f;   // 100000000
```

Arithmetic Operators

The arithmetic operators (+, -, *, /, %) are defined for all numeric types except the 8- and 16-bit integral types. The % operator evaluates the remainder after division.

Increment and Decrement Operators

The increment and decrement operators (++, --, respectively) increment and decrement numeric types by 1. The operator can either precede or follow the variable, depending on whether you want the variable to be updated *before* or *after* the expression is evaluated. For example:

```
int x = 0;
Console.WriteLine (x++);   // Outputs 0; x is now 1
Console.WriteLine (++x);   // Outputs 2; x is now 2
Console.WriteLine (--x);   // Outputs 1; x is now 1
```

Specialized Integral Operations

Division

Division operations on integral types always truncate remainders (round toward zero). Dividing by a variable whose value is zero generates a runtime error (a DivideByZeroException). Dividing by the *literal* or *constant* 0 generates a compile-time error.

Overflow

At runtime, arithmetic operations on integral types can overflow. By default, this happens silently—no exception is thrown and the result exhibits wraparound behavior, as though the computation were done on a larger integer type and the extra significant bits discarded. For example, decrementing the minimum possible int value results in the maximum possible int value:

```
int a = int.MinValue; a--;
Console.WriteLine (a == int.MaxValue); // True
```

The checked and unchecked operators

The checked operator instructs the runtime to generate an Over flowException rather than overflowing silently when an integral-typed expression or statement exceeds the arithmetic limits of that type. The checked operator affects expressions with the ++, --, (unary) -, +, -, *, /, and explicit conversion operators between integral types. Overflow checking incurs a small performance cost.

You can use checked around either an expression or a statement block. For example:

```
int a = 1000000, b = 1000000;

int c = checked (a * b);   // Checks just the expression

checked                    // Checks all expressions
{                          // in statement block.
   c = a * b;
   ...
}
```

You can make arithmetic overflow checking the default for all expressions in a program by compiling with the /checked+ command-line switch (in Visual Studio, go to Advanced Build Settings). If you then need to disable overflow checking just for specific expressions or statements, you can do so with the unchecked operator.

Bitwise operators

C# supports the following bitwise operators:

Operator	Meaning	Sample expression	Result
~	Complement	~0xfU	0xfffffff0U
&	And	0xf0 & 0x33	0x30
|	Or	0xf0 | 0x33	0xf3
^	Exclusive Or	0xff00 ^ 0x0ff0	0xf0f0
<<	Shift left	0x20 << 2	0x80
>>	Shift right	0x20 >> 1	0x10

8- and 16-Bit Integral Types

The 8- and 16-bit integral types are byte, sbyte, short, and ushort. These types lack their own arithmetic operators, so C# implicitly converts them to larger types as required. This can cause a compilation error when trying to assign the result back to a small integral type:

```
short x = 1, y = 1;
short z = x + y;          // Compile-time error
```

In this case, x and y are implicitly converted to int so that the addition can be performed. This means that the result is also an int, which cannot be implicitly cast back to a short (because it could cause loss of data). To make this compile, we must add an explicit cast:

```
short z = (short) (x + y);   // OK
```

Special Float and Double Values

Unlike integral types, floating-point types have values that certain operations treat specially. These special values are NaN (Not a Number), $+\infty$, $-\infty$, and -0. The float and double classes have constants for NaN, $+\infty$, and $-\infty$ (as well as other values including MaxValue, MinValue, and Epsilon). For example:

```
Console.Write (double.NegativeInfinity);   // -Infinity
```

Dividing a nonzero number by zero results in an infinite value:

```
Console.WriteLine ( 1.0 /  0.0);   //  Infinity
Console.WriteLine (-1.0 /  0.0);   // -Infinity
Console.WriteLine ( 1.0 / -0.0);   // -Infinity
Console.WriteLine (-1.0 / -0.0);   //  Infinity
```

Dividing zero by zero, or subtracting infinity from infinity, results in a NaN:

```
Console.Write ( 0.0 / 0.0);                  // NaN
Console.Write ((1.0 / 0.0) - (1.0 / 0.0));   // NaN
```

When you use ==, a NaN value is never equal to another value, even another NaN value. To test whether a value is NaN, you must use the float.IsNaN or double.IsNaN method:

```
Console.WriteLine (0.0 / 0.0 == double.NaN);   // False
Console.WriteLine (double.IsNaN (0.0 / 0.0));   // True
```

When you use object.Equals, however, two NaN values are equal:

```
bool isTrue = object.Equals (0.0/0.0, double.NaN);
```

double versus decimal

double is useful for scientific computations (such as computing spatial coordinates). decimal is useful for financial computations and values that are "man-made" rather than the result of real-world measurements. Here's a summary of the differences:

Feature	double	decimal
Internal representation	Base 2	Base 10
Precision	15–16 significant figures	28–29 significant figures
Range	$\pm(\sim 10^{-324}$ to $\sim 10^{308})$	$\pm(\sim 10^{-28}$ to $\sim 10^{28})$
Special values	$+0, -0, +\infty, -\infty,$ and NaN	None

Feature	double	decimal
Speed	Native to processor	Non-native to processor (about 10 times slower than double)

Real Number Rounding Errors

float and double internally represent numbers in base 2. For this reason, most literals with a fractional component (which are in base 10) will not be represented precisely:

```
float tenth = 0.1f;                      // Not quite 0.1
float one   = 1f;
Console.WriteLine (one - tenth * 10f);   // -1.490116E-08
```

This is why float and double are bad for financial calculations. In contrast, decimal works in base 10 and so can precisely represent fractional numbers such as 0.1 (whose base-10 representation is nonrecurring).

Boolean Type and Operators

C#'s bool type (aliasing the System.Boolean type) is a logical value that can be assigned the literal true or false.

Although a Boolean value requires only one bit of storage, the runtime will use one byte of memory because this is the minimum chunk that the runtime and processor can efficiently work with. To avoid space inefficiency in the case of arrays, .NET provides a BitArray class in the System.Collec tions namespace that is designed to use just one bit per Boolean value.

Equality and Comparison Operators

== and != test for equality and inequality, respectively, of any type, and always return a bool value. Value types typically have a very simple notion of equality:

```
int x = 1, y = 2, z = 1;
Console.WriteLine (x == y);     // False
Console.WriteLine (x == z);     // True
```

For reference types, equality, by default, is based on *reference*, as opposed to the actual *value* of the underlying object. Therefore, two instances of an object with identical data are not considered equal unless the == operator for that type is specially overloaded to that effect (see "The object Type" on page 91 and "Operator Overloading" on page 196).

The equality and comparison operators, ==, !=, <, >, >=, and <=, work for all numeric types, but should be used with caution with real numbers (see "Real Number Rounding Errors" on page 25 in the previous section). The comparison operators also work on enum type members, by comparing their underlying integral values.

Conditional Operators

The && and || operators test for *and* and *or* conditions, respectively. They are frequently used in conjunction with the ! operator, which expresses *not*. In the following example, the UseUm brella method returns true if it's rainy or sunny (to protect us from the rain or the sun), as long as it's not also windy (because umbrellas are useless in the wind):

```
static bool UseUmbrella (bool rainy, bool sunny,
                         bool windy)
{
  return !windy && (rainy || sunny);
}
```

The && and || operators *short-circuit* evaluation when possible. In the preceding example, if it is windy, the expression (rainy || sunny) is not even evaluated. Short-circuiting is essential in allowing expressions such as the following to run without throwing a NullReferenceException:

```
if (sb != null && sb.Length > 0) ...
```

The & and | operators also test for *and* and *or* conditions:

```
    return !windy & (rainy | sunny);
```

The difference is that they *do not short-circuit*. For this reason, they are rarely used in place of conditional operators.

The ternary conditional operator (simply called the *conditional operator*) has the form q ? a : b, where if condition q is true, a is evaluated, else b is evaluated. For example:

```
static int Max (int a, int b)
{
  return (a > b) ? a : b;
}
```

The conditional operator is particularly useful in LINQ queries.

Strings and Characters

C#'s char type (aliasing the System.Char type) represents a Unicode character and occupies two bytes (UTF-16). A char literal is specified inside single quotes:

```
char c = 'A';       // Simple character
```

Escape sequences express characters that cannot be expressed or interpreted literally. An escape sequence is a backslash followed by a character with a special meaning. For example:

```
char newLine = '\n';
char backSlash = '\\';
```

The escape sequence characters are as follows:

Char	Meaning	Value
\'	Single quote	0x0027
\"	Double quote	0x0022
\\	Backslash	0x005C
\0	Null	0x0000
\a	Alert	0x0007
\b	Backspace	0x0008

Char	Meaning	Value
\f	Form feed	0x000C
\n	New line	0x000A
\r	Carriage return	0x000D
\t	Horizontal tab	0x0009
\v	Vertical tab	0x000B

The \u (or \x) escape sequence lets you specify any Unicode character via its four-digit hexadecimal code:

```
char copyrightSymbol = '\u00A9';
char omegaSymbol     = '\u03A9';
char newLine         = '\u000A';
```

An implicit conversion from a char to a numeric type works for the numeric types that can accommodate an unsigned short. For other numeric types, an explicit conversion is required.

String Type

C#'s string type (aliasing the System.String type) represents an immutable (unmodifiable) sequence of Unicode characters. A string literal is specified within double quotes:

```
string a = "Heat";
```

NOTE

string is a reference type rather than a value type. Its equality operators, however, follow value type semantics:

```
string a = "test", b = "test";
Console.Write (a == b);  // True
```

The escape sequences that are valid for char literals also work within strings:

```
string a = "Here's a tab:\t";
```

The cost of this is that whenever you need a literal backslash, you must write it twice:

```
string a1 = "\\\\server\\fileshare\\helloworld.cs";
```

To avoid this problem, C# allows *verbatim* string literals. A verbatim string literal is prefixed with @ and does not support escape sequences. The following verbatim string is identical to the preceding one:

```
string a2 = @"\\server\fileshare\helloworld.cs";
```

A verbatim string literal can also span multiple lines. You can include the double-quote character in a verbatim literal by writing it twice.

String concatenation

The + operator concatenates two strings:

```
string s = "a" + "b";
```

One of the operands can be a nonstring value, in which case ToString is called on that value. For example:

```
string s = "a" + 5;  // a5
```

Using the + operator repeatedly to build up a string can be inefficient: a better solution is to use the System.Text.String Builder type—this represents a mutable (editable) string, and has methods to efficiently Append, Insert, Remove, and Replace substrings.

String interpolation

A string preceded with the $ character is called an *interpolated string*. Interpolated strings can include expressions within braces:

```
int x = 4;
Console.Write ($"A square has {x} sides");
// Prints: A square has 4 sides
```

Any valid C# expression of any type can appear within the braces, and C# will convert the expression to a string by calling its `ToString` method or equivalent. You can change the formatting by appending the expression with a colon and a *format string* (we describe format strings in Chapter 6 of *C# 8.0 in a Nutshell*):

```
string s = $"15 in hex is {15:X2}";
// Evaluates to "15 in hex is 0F"
```

Interpolated strings must complete on a single line, unless you also specify the verbatim string operator. Note that the $ operator must come before @:

```
int x = 2;
string s = $@"this spans {
x} lines";
```

To include a brace literal in an interpolated string, repeat the desired brace character.

String comparisons

`string` does not support `<` and `>` operators for comparisons. You must instead use `string`'s `CompareTo` method, which returns a positive number, a negative number, or zero, depending on whether the first value comes after, before, or alongside the second value:

```
Console.Write ("Boston".CompareTo ("Austin"));   // 1
Console.Write ("Boston".CompareTo ("Boston"));   // 0
Console.Write ("Boston".CompareTo ("Chicago"));  // -1
```

Searching within strings

`string`'s indexer returns a character at a specified position:

```
Console.Write ("word"[2]);   // r
```

The `IndexOf` and `LastIndexOf` methods search for a character within the string. The `Contains`, `StartsWith`, and `EndsWith` methods search for a substring within the string.

Manipulating strings

Because `string` is immutable, all the methods that "manipulate" a string return a new one, leaving the original untouched:

- `Substring` extracts a portion of a string.
- `Insert` and `Remove` insert and remove characters at a specified position.
- `PadLeft` and `PadRight` add whitespace.
- `TrimStart`, `TrimEnd`, and `Trim` remove whitespace.

The `string` class also defines `ToUpper` and `ToLower` methods for changing case, a `Split` method to split a string into substrings (based on supplied delimiters), and a static `Join` method to join substrings back into a string.

Arrays

An array represents a fixed number of elements of a particular type. The elements in an array are always stored in a contiguous block of memory, providing highly efficient access.

An array is denoted with square brackets after the element type. The following declares an array of five characters:

```
char[] vowels = new char[5];
```

Square brackets also *index* the array, accessing a particular element by position:

```
vowels[0] = 'a'; vowels[1] = 'e'; vowels[2] = 'i';
vowels[3] = 'o'; vowels[4] = 'u';

Console.WriteLine (vowels [1]);        // e
```

This prints "e" because array indexes start at 0. We can use a `for` loop statement to iterate through each element in the array. The for loop in this example cycles the integer `i` from 0 to 4:

```
for (int i = 0; i < vowels.Length; i++)
  Console.Write (vowels [i]);          // aeiou
```

Arrays also implement IEnumerable<T> (see "Enumeration and Iterators" on page 144), so you can also enumerate members with the foreach statement:

```
foreach (char c in vowels) Console.Write (c);   // aeiou
```

All array indexing is bounds-checked by the runtime. An Index OutOfRangeException is thrown if you use an invalid index:

```
vowels[5] = 'y';   // Runtime error
```

The Length property of an array returns the number of elements in the array. After an array has been created, its length cannot be changed. The System.Collection namespace and subnamespaces provide higher-level data structures, such as dynamically sized arrays and dictionaries.

An *array initialization expression* lets you declare and populate an array in a single step:

```
char[] vowels = new char[] {'a','e','i','o','u'};
```

or simply:

```
char[] vowels = {'a','e','i','o','u'};
```

All arrays inherit from the System.Array class, which defines common methods and properties for all arrays. This includes instance properties such as Length and Rank, and static methods to do the following:

- Dynamically create an array (CreateInstance)

- Get and set elements regardless of the array type (Get Value/SetValue)

- Search a sorted array (BinarySearch) or an unsorted array (IndexOf, LastIndexOf, Find, FindIndex, FindLast Index)

- Sort an array (Sort)

- Copy an array (Copy)

Default Element Initialization

Creating an array always preinitializes the elements with default values. The default value for a type is the result of a bit-wise zeroing of memory. For example, consider creating an array of integers. Because int is a value type, this allocates 1,000 integers in one contiguous block of memory. The default value for each element will be 0:

```
int[] a = new int[1000];
Console.Write (a[123]);          // 0
```

With reference type elements, the default value is null.

An array *itself* is always a reference type object, regardless of element type. For instance, the following is legal:

```
int[] a = null;
```

Indices and Ranges (C# 8)

C# 8 introduces *indices* and *ranges* to simplify working with elements or portions of an array.

NOTE

Indices and ranges also work with the CLR types Span<T> and ReadOnlySpan<T>, which provide efficient low-level access to managed or unmanaged memory.

You can also make your own types work with indices and ranges, by defining an indexer of type Index or Range (see "Indexers" on page 78).

Indices

Indices let you refer to elements relative to the *end* of an array, with the ^ operator. ^1 refers to the last element, ^2 refers to the second-to-last element, and so on:

```
char[] vowels = new char[] {'a','e','i','o','u'};
char lastElement  = vowels[^1];   // 'u'
char secondToLast = vowels[^2];   // 'o'
```

(^0 equals the length of the array, so vowels[^0] generates an error.)

C# implements indices with the help of the Index type, so you can also do the following:

```
Index first = 0;
Index last = ^1;
char firstElement = vowels [first];   // 'a'
char lastElement  = vowels [last];    // 'u'
```

Ranges

Ranges let you "slice" an array with the .. operator:

```
char[] firstTwo  = vowels [..2];   // 'a', 'e'
char[] lastThree = vowels [2..];   // 'i', 'o', 'u'
char[] middleOne = vowels [2..3]   // 'i'
```

The second number in the range is *exclusive*, so ..2 returns the elements *before* vowels[2].

You can also use the ^ symbol in ranges. The following returns the last two characters:

```
char[] lastTwo = vowels [^2..^0];   // 'o', 'u'
```

(^0 is valid here because the second number in the range is *exclusive*.)

C# implements ranges with the help of the Range type, so you can also do the following:

```
Range firstTwoRange = 0..2;
char[] firstTwo = vowels [firstTwoRange];   // 'a', 'e'
```

Multidimensional Arrays

Multidimensional arrays come in two varieties: *rectangular* and *jagged*. Rectangular arrays represent an *n*-dimensional block of memory, and jagged arrays are arrays of arrays.

Rectangular arrays

To declare rectangular arrays, use commas to separate each dimension. The following declares a rectangular two-dimensional array, where the dimensions are 3 × 3:

```
int[,] matrix = new int [3, 3];
```

The GetLength method of an array returns the length for a given dimension (starting at 0):

```
for (int i = 0; i < matrix.GetLength(0); i++)
  for (int j = 0; j < matrix.GetLength(1); j++)
    matrix [i, j] = i * 3 + j;
```

A rectangular array can be initialized as follows (to create an array identical to the previous example):

```
int[,] matrix = new int[,]
{
  {0,1,2},
  {3,4,5},
  {6,7,8}
};
```

(The code shown in boldface can be omitted in declaration statements such as this.)

Jagged arrays

To declare jagged arrays, use successive square-bracket pairs for each dimension. Here is an example of declaring a jagged two-dimensional array, for which the outermost dimension is 3:

```
int[][] matrix = new int[3][];
```

The inner dimensions aren't specified in the declaration because, unlike a rectangular array, each inner array can be an arbitrary length. Each inner array is implicitly initialized to null rather than an empty array. Each inner array must be created manually:

```
for (int i = 0; i < matrix.Length; i++)
{
  matrix[i] = new int [3];        // Create inner array
  for (int j = 0; j < matrix[i].Length; j++)
    matrix[i][j] = i * 3 + j;
}
```

A jagged array can be initialized as follows (to create an array identical to the previous example, but with an additional element at the end):

```
int[][] matrix = new int[][]
{
  new int[] {0,1,2},
  new int[] {3,4,5},
  new int[] {6,7,8,9}
};
```

(The code shown in boldface can be omitted in declaration statements such as this.)

Simplified Array Initialization Expressions

We've already seen how to simplify array initialization expressions by omitting the new keyword and type declaration:

```
char[] vowels = new char[] {'a','e','i','o','u'};
char[] vowels =              {'a','e','i','o','u'};
```

Another approach is to omit the type name after the new keyword, and have the compiler *infer* the array type. This is a useful shortcut when you're passing arrays as arguments. For example, consider the following method:

```
void Foo (char[] data) { ... }
```

We can call this method with an array that we create on the fly, as follows:

```
Foo ( new char[] {'a','e','i','o','u'} );      // Longhand
Foo ( new[]       {'a','e','i','o','u'} );   // Shortcut
```

This shortcut is essential in creating arrays of *anonymous types*, as you'll see later.

Variables and Parameters

A variable represents a storage location that has a modifiable value. A variable can be a *local variable*, *parameter* (*value*, *ref*, *out*, or *in*), *field* (*instance* or *static*), or *array element*.

The Stack and the Heap

The stack and the heap are the places where variables reside. Each has very different lifetime semantics.

Stack

The stack is a block of memory for storing local variables and parameters. The stack logically grows and shrinks as a method or function is entered and exited. Consider the following method (to avoid distraction, input argument checking is ignored):

```
static int Factorial (int x)
{
  if (x == 0) return 1;
  return x * Factorial (x-1);
}
```

This method is *recursive*, meaning that it calls itself. Each time the method is entered, a new int is allocated on the stack, and each time the method exits, the int is deallocated.

Heap

The heap is the memory in which *objects* (i.e., reference type instances) reside. Whenever a new object is created, it is allocated on the heap, and a reference to that object is returned. During a program's execution, the heap starts filling up as new objects are created. The runtime has a garbage collector that periodically deallocates objects from the heap, so your program does not run out of memory. An object is eligible for deallocation as soon as it's not referenced by anything that is itself alive.

Value type instances (and object references) live wherever the variable was declared. If the instance was declared as a field within a class type, or as an array element, that instance lives on the heap.

NOTE

You can't explicitly delete objects in C#, as you can in C++. An unreferenced object is eventually collected by the garbage collector.

The heap also stores static fields and constants. Unlike objects allocated on the heap (which can be garbage-collected), these live until the application domain is torn down.

Definite Assignment

C# enforces a definite assignment policy. In practice, this means that outside of an `unsafe` context, it's impossible to access uninitialized memory. Definite assignment has three implications:

- Local variables must be assigned a value before they can be read.

- Function arguments must be supplied when a method is called (unless marked optional—see "Optional parameters" on page 43).

- All other variables (such as fields and array elements) are automatically initialized by the runtime.

For example, the following code results in a compile-time error:

```
static void Main()
{
  int x;
  Console.WriteLine (x);        // Compile-time error
}
```

However, if x were instead a *field* of the containing class, this would be legal and would print 0.

Default Values

All type instances have a default value. The default value for the predefined types is the result of a bitwise zeroing of memory, and is null for reference types, 0 for numeric and enum types, '\0' for the char type, and false for the bool type.

You can obtain the default value for any type by using the default keyword (this is particularly useful with generics, as you'll see later). The default value in a custom value type (i.e., struct) is the same as the default value for each field defined by the custom type.

Parameters

A method can have a sequence of parameters. Parameters define the set of arguments that must be provided for that method. In this example, the method Foo has a single parameter named p, of type int:

```
static void Foo (int p)    // p is a parameter
{
    ...
}
static void Main() { Foo (8); }    // 8 is an argument
```

You can control how parameters are passed with the ref, out, and in modifiers:

Parameter modifier	Passed by	Variable must be definitely assigned
None	Value	Going *in*
ref	Reference	Going *in*
out	Reference	Going *out*
in	Reference (read-only)	Going *in*

Passing arguments by value

By default, arguments in C# are *passed by value*, which is by far the most common case. This means that a copy of the value is created when it is passed to the method:

```
static void Foo (int p)
{
  p = p + 1;                  // Increment p by 1
  Console.WriteLine (p);      // Write p to screen
}
static void Main()
{
  int x = 8;
  Foo (x);                    // Make a copy of x
  Console.WriteLine (x);      // x will still be 8
}
```

Assigning p a new value does not change the contents of x, because p and x reside in different memory locations.

Passing a reference type argument by value copies the *reference* but not the object. In the following example, Foo sees the same StringBuilder object that Main instantiated, but has an independent *reference* to it. In other words, sb and fooSB are separate variables that reference the same StringBuilder object:

```
static void Foo (StringBuilder fooSB)
{
  fooSB.Append ("test");
  fooSB = null;
}
static void Main()
{
  StringBuilder sb = new StringBuilder();
  Foo (sb);
  Console.WriteLine (sb.ToString());   // test
}
```

Because fooSB is a *copy* of a reference, setting it to null doesn't make sb null. (If, however, fooSB was declared and called with the ref modifier, sb *would* become null.)

The ref modifier

To *pass by reference*, C# provides the ref parameter modifier. In the following example, p and x refer to the same memory locations:

```
static void Foo (ref int p)
{
  p = p + 1;
  Console.WriteLine (p);
}
static void Main()
{
  int x = 8;
  Foo (ref x);              // Pass x by reference
  Console.WriteLine (x);    // x is now 9
}
```

Now assigning p a new value changes the contents of x. Notice how the ref modifier is required both when writing and calling the method. This makes it very clear what's going on.

NOTE

A parameter can be passed by reference or by value, regardless of whether the parameter type is a reference type or a value type.

The out modifier

An out argument is like a ref argument, except for the following:

- It need not be assigned before going into the function.
- It must be assigned before it comes *out* of the function.

The out modifier is most commonly used to get multiple return values back from a method.

Out variables and discards

From C# 7, you can declare variables on the fly when calling methods with out parameters:

```
int.TryParse ("123", out int x);
Console.WriteLine (x);
```

This is equivalent to:

```
int x;
int.TryParse ("123", out x);
Console.WriteLine (x);
```

When calling methods with multiple out parameters, you can use an underscore to "discard" any in which you're uninterested. Assuming SomeBigMethod has been defined with five out parameters, you can ignore all but the third, as follows:

```
SomeBigMethod (out _, out _, out int x, out _, out _);
Console.WriteLine (x);
```

The in modifier

From C# 7.2, you can prefix a parameter with the in modifier to prevent it from being modified within the method. This allows the compiler to avoid the overhead of copying the argument prior to passing it in, which can matter in the case of large custom value types (see "Structs" on page 96).

The params modifier

The params modifier, if applied to the last parameter of a method, allows the method to accept any number of arguments of a particular type. The parameter type must be declared as an array. For example:

```
static int Sum (params int[] ints)
{
  int sum = 0;
  for (int i = 0; i < ints.Length; i++) sum += ints[i];
  return sum;
}
```

You can call this as follows:

```
Console.WriteLine (Sum (1, 2, 3, 4));    // 10
```

You can also supply a `params` argument as an ordinary array. The preceding call is semantically equivalent to:

```
Console.WriteLine (Sum (new int[] { 1, 2, 3, 4 } ));
```

Optional parameters

Methods, constructors, and indexers can declare *optional parameters*. A parameter is optional if it specifies a *default value* in its declaration:

```
void Foo (int x = 23) { Console.WriteLine (x); }
```

You can omit optional parameters when calling the method:

```
Foo();    // 23
```

The *default argument* of 23 is actually *passed* to the optional parameter x—the compiler bakes the value 23 into the compiled code at the *calling* side. The preceding call to Foo is semantically identical to

```
Foo (23);
```

because the compiler simply substitutes the default value of an optional parameter wherever it is used.

NOTE

Adding an optional parameter to a public method that's called from another assembly requires recompilation of both assemblies—just as though the parameter were mandatory.

The default value of an optional parameter must be specified by a constant expression, or a parameterless constructor of a value type. You cannot mark optional parameters with `ref` or `out`.

Mandatory parameters must occur *before* optional parameters in both the method declaration and the method call (the exception is with params arguments, which still always come last). In the following example, the explicit value of 1 is passed to x, and the default value of 0 is passed to y:

```
void Foo (int x = 0, int y = 0)
{
  Console.WriteLine (x + ", " + y);
}
void Test()
{
  Foo(1);     // 1, 0
}
```

To do the converse (pass a default value to x and an explicit value to y), you must combine optional parameters with *named arguments*.

Named arguments

Rather than identifying an argument by position, you can identify an argument by name. For example:

```
void Foo (int x, int y)
{
  Console.WriteLine (x + ", " + y);
}
void Test()
{
  Foo (x:1, y:2);  // 1, 2
}
```

Named arguments can occur in any order. The following calls to Foo are semantically identical:

```
Foo (x:1, y:2);
Foo (y:2, x:1);
```

You can mix named and positional arguments, as long as the named arguments appear last:

```
Foo (1, y:2);
```

Named arguments are particularly useful in conjunction with optional parameters. For instance, consider the following method:

```
void Bar (int a=0, int b=0, int c=0, int d=0) { ... }
```

We can call this, supplying only a value for d, as follows:

```
Bar (d:3);
```

This is particularly useful when you're calling COM APIs.

var—Implicitly Typed Local Variables

It is often the case that you declare and initialize a variable in
one step. If the compiler is able to infer the type from the initialization expression, you can use the word var in place of the
type declaration. For example:

```
var x = "hello";
var y = new System.Text.StringBuilder();
var z = (float)Math.PI;
```

This is precisely equivalent to the following:

```
string x = "hello";
System.Text.StringBuilder y =
  new System.Text.StringBuilder();
float z = (float)Math.PI;
```

Because of this direct equivalence, implicitly typed variables are
statically typed. For example, the following generates a
compile-time error:

```
var x = 5;
x = "hello";   // Compile-time error; x is of type int
```

In the section "Anonymous Types" on page 158, we describe a
scenario in which the use of var is mandatory.

Expressions and Operators

An *expression* essentially denotes a value. The simplest kinds of
expressions are constants (such as 123) and variables (such as
x). Expressions can be transformed and combined with operators. An *operator* takes one or more input *operands* to output a
new expression:

```
12 * 30   // * is an operator; 12 and 30 are operands.
```

Complex expressions can be built because an operand can itself be an expression, such as the operand (12 * 30) in the following example:

```
1 + (12 * 30)
```

Operators in C# can be classed as *unary*, *binary*, or *ternary*, depending on the number of operands they work on (one, two, or three). The binary operators always use *infix* notation, in which the operator is placed *between* the two operands.

Operators that are intrinsic to the basic plumbing of the language are called *primary*; an example is the method call operator. An expression that has no value is called a *void expression*:

```
Console.WriteLine (1)
```

Because a void expression has no value, you cannot use it as an operand to build more complex expressions:

```
1 + Console.WriteLine (1)      // Compile-time error
```

Assignment Expressions

An assignment expression uses the = operator to assign the result of another expression to a variable. For example:

```
x = x * 5
```

An assignment expression is not a void expression. It actually carries the assignment value, and so can be incorporated into another expression. In the following example, the expression assigns 2 to x and 10 to y:

```
y = 5 * (x = 2)
```

This style of expression can be used to initialize multiple values:

```
a = b = c = d = 0
```

The *compound assignment operators* are syntactic shortcuts that combine assignment with another operator. For example:

```
x *= 2     // equivalent to x = x * 2
x <<= 1    // equivalent to x = x << 1
```

(A subtle exception to this rule is with *events*, which we describe later: the += and -= operators here are treated specially and map to the event's add and remove accessors, respectively.)

Operator Precedence and Associativity

When an expression contains multiple operators, *precedence* and *associativity* determine the order of their evaluation. Operators with higher precedence execute before operators of lower precedence. If the operators have the same precedence, the operator's associativity determines the order of evaluation.

Precedence

The expression 1 + 2 * 3 is evaluated as 1 + (2 * 3) because * has a higher precedence than +.

Left-associative operators

Binary operators (except for assignment, lambda, and null-coalescing operators) are *left-associative*; in other words, they are evaluated from left to right. For example, the expression 8/4/2 is evaluated as (8/4)/2 due to left associativity. Of course, you can insert your own parentheses to change evaluation order.

Right-associative operators

The *assignment and lambda operators*, null-coalescing operator, and (ternary) conditional operator are *right-associative*; in other words, they are evaluated from right to left. Right associativity allows multiple assignments such as x=y=3 to compile: it works by first assigning 3 to y and then assigning the result of that expression (3) to x.

Operator Table

The following table lists C#'s operators in order of precedence. Operators listed under the same subheading have the same precedence. We explain user-overloadable operators in "Operator Overloading" on page 196.

Operator symbol	Operator name	Example	Overloadable
Primary (highest precedence)			
.	Member access	x.y	No
?.	Null-conditional	x?.y	No
->	Pointer to struct (unsafe)	x->y	No
()	Function call	x()	No
[]	Array/index	a[x]	Via indexer
++	Post-increment	x++	Yes
--	Post-decrement	x--	Yes
new	Create instance	new Foo()	No
stackalloc	Unsafe stack allocation	stackalloc(10)	No
typeof	Get type from identifier	typeof(int)	No
nameof	Get name of identifier	nameof(x)	No
checked	Integral overflow check on	checked(x)	No
unchecked	Integral overflow check off	unchecked(x)	No
default	Default value	default(char)	No
sizeof	Get size of struct	sizeof(int)	No
Unary			
await	Await	await myTask	No
+	Positive value of	+x	Yes
-	Negative value of	-x	Yes

Operator symbol	Operator name	Example	Overloadable
!	Not	!x	Yes
~	Bitwise complement	~x	Yes
++	Pre-increment	++x	Yes
--	Pre-decrement	--x	Yes
()	Cast	(int)x	No
*	Value at address (unsafe)	*x	No
&	Address of value (unsafe)	&x	No
Multiplicative			
*	Multiply	x * y	Yes
/	Divide	x / y	Yes
%	Remainder	x % y	Yes
Additive			
+	Add	x + y	Yes
-	Subtract	x - y	Yes
Shift			
<<	Shift left	x << 1	Yes
>>	Shift right	x >> 1	Yes
Relational			
<	Less than	x < y	Yes
>	Greater than	x > y	Yes
<=	Less than or equal to	x <= y	Yes
>=	Greater than or equal to	x >= y	Yes
is	Type is or is subclass of	x is y	No

Operator symbol	Operator name	Example	Overloadable
as	Type conversion	x as y	No
Equality			
==	Equals	x == y	Yes
!=	Not equals	x != y	Yes
Logical And			
&	And	x & y	Yes
Logical Xor			
^	Exclusive Or	x ^ y	Yes
Logical Or			
		Or	x	y	Yes
Conditional And			
&&	Conditional And	x && y	Via &
Conditional Or			
||	Conditional Or	x || y	Via	
Null coalescing			
??	Null coalescing	x ?? y	No
Conditional (Ternary)			
? :	Conditional	isTrue ? thenThis : elseThis	No
Assignment and lambda (lowest precedence)			
=	Assign	x = y	No
*=	Multiply self by	x *= 2	Via *
/=	Divide self by	x /= 2	Via /
+=	Add to self	x += 2	Via +
-=	Subtract from self	x -= 2	Via -

Operator symbol	Operator name	Example	Overloadable
<<=	Shift self left by	x <<= 2	Via <<
>>=	Shift self right by	x >>= 2	Via >>
&=	And self by	x &= 2	Via &
^=	Exclusive-Or self by	x ^= 2	Via ^
|=	Or self by	x |= 2	Via |
=>	Lambda	x => x + 1	No

Null Operators

C# provides three operators to make it easier to work with nulls: the *null-coalescing operator*, the *null-conditional operator*, and the *null-coalescing assignment operator*.

Null-Coalescing Operator

The ?? operator is the *null-coalescing operator*. It says, "If the operand to the left is non-null, give it to me; otherwise, give me another value." For example:

```
string s1 = null;
string s2 = s1 ?? "nothing"; // s2 evaluates to "nothing"
```

If the left-hand expression is non-null, the righthand expression is never evaluated. The null-coalescing operator also works with nullable value types (see "Nullable (Value) Types" on page 149).

Null-Conditional Operator

The ?. operator is the *null-conditional* or "Elvis" operator, and was introduced in C# 6. It allows you to call methods and access members just like the standard dot operator, except that if the operand on the left is null, the expression evaluates to null instead of throwing a NullReferenceException:

```
System.Text.StringBuilder sb = null;
string s = sb?.ToString();   // No error; s is null
```

The last line is equivalent to this:

```
string s = (sb == null ? null : sb.ToString());
```

Upon encountering a null, the Elvis operator short-circuits the remainder of the expression. In the following example, s evaluates to null, even with a standard dot operator between ToString() and ToUpper():

```
System.Text.StringBuilder sb = null;
string s = sb?.ToString().ToUpper();   // No error
```

Repeated use of Elvis is necessary only if the operand immediately to its left might be null. The following expression is robust to both x being null and x.y being null:

```
x?.y?.z
```

and is equivalent to the following (except that x.y is evaluated only once):

```
x == null ? null
          : (x.y == null ? null : x.y.z)
```

The final expression must be capable of accepting a null. The following is illegal because int cannot accept a null:

```
System.Text.StringBuilder sb = null;
int length = sb?.ToString().Length;   // Illegal
```

We can fix this with the use of nullable value types (see "Nullable (Value) Types" on page 149):

```
int? length = sb?.ToString().Length;   // OK : int? can
be null
```

You can also use the null-conditional operator to call a void method:

```
someObject?.SomeVoidMethod();
```

If someObject is null, this becomes a "no-operation" rather than throwing a NullReferenceException.

The null-conditional operator can be used with the commonly used type members that we describe in "Classes" on page 67, including *methods*, *fields*, *properties*, and *indexers*. It also combines well with the *null-coalescing operator*:

```
System.Text.StringBuilder sb = null;
string s = sb?.ToString() ?? "nothing";   // s evaluates
to "nothing"
```

Null-Coalescing Assignment (C# 8)

The ??= operator assigns a variable only if it's not null. Instead of this:

```
if (s != null) s = "Hello, world";
```

you can now write this:

```
s ??= "Hello, world";
```

Statements

Functions comprise statements that execute sequentially in the textual order in which they appear. A *statement block* is a series of statements appearing between braces (the {} tokens).

Declaration Statements

A declaration statement declares a new variable, optionally initializing the variable with an expression. A declaration statement ends in a semicolon. You can declare multiple variables of the same type in a comma-separated list. For example:

```
bool rich = true, famous = false;
```

A constant declaration is like a variable declaration, except that it cannot be changed after it has been declared, and the initialization must occur with the declaration (more on this in "Constants" on page 68):

```
const double c = 2.99792458E08;
```

Local variable scope

The scope of a local variable or local constant variable extends throughout the current block. You cannot declare another local variable with the same name in the current block or in any nested blocks.

Expression Statements

Expression statements are expressions that are also valid statements. In practice, this means expressions that "do" something; in other words:

- Instantiate an object
- Call a method

Expressions that do none of these are not valid statements:

```
string s = "foo";
s.Length;          // Illegal statement: does nothing!
```

When you call a constructor or a method that returns a value, you're not obliged to use the result. However, unless the constructor or method changes state, the statement is useless:

```
new StringBuilder();    // Legal, but useless
x.Equals (y);           // Legal, but useless
```

Selection Statements

Selection statements conditionally control the flow of program execution.

The if statement

An if statement executes a statement if a bool expression is true. For example:

```
if (5 < 2 * 3)
  Console.WriteLine ("true");      // true
```

The statement can be a code block:

```
if (5 < 2 * 3)
{
  Console.WriteLine ("true");        // true
  Console.WriteLine ("...")
}
```

The else clause

An if statement can optionally feature an else clause:

```
if (2 + 2 == 5)
  Console.WriteLine ("Does not compute");
else
  Console.WriteLine ("False");       // False
```

Within an else clause, you can nest another if statement:

```
if (2 + 2 == 5)
  Console.WriteLine ("Does not compute");
else
  if (2 + 2 == 4)
    Console.WriteLine ("Computes");   // Computes
```

Changing the flow of execution with braces

An else clause always applies to the immediately preceding if statement in the statement block. For example:

```
if (true)
  if (false)
    Console.WriteLine();
  else
    Console.WriteLine ("executes");
```

This is semantically identical to the following:

```
if (true)
{
  if (false)
    Console.WriteLine();
  else
    Console.WriteLine ("executes");
}
```

We can change the execution flow by moving the braces:

```
if (true)
{
```

```
    if (false)
      Console.WriteLine();
  }
  else
    Console.WriteLine ("does not execute");
```

C# has no "elseif" keyword; however, the following pattern achieves the same result:

```
static void TellMeWhatICanDo (int age)
{
  if (age >= 35)
    Console.WriteLine ("You can be president!");
  else if (age >= 21)
    Console.WriteLine ("You can drink!");
  else if (age >= 18)
    Console.WriteLine ("You can vote!");
  else
    Console.WriteLine ("You can wait!");
}
```

The switch statement

switch statements let you branch program execution based on a selection of possible values that a variable might have. switch statements can result in cleaner code than multiple if statements because switch statements require an expression to be evaluated only once. For instance:

```
static void ShowCard (int cardNumber)
{
  switch (cardNumber)
  {
    case 13:
      Console.WriteLine ("King");
      break;
    case 12:
      Console.WriteLine ("Queen");
      break;
    case 11:
      Console.WriteLine ("Jack");
      break;
    default:    // Any other cardNumber
      Console.WriteLine (cardNumber);
      break;
```

```
    }
}
```

The values in each case expression must be constants, which restricts their allowable types to the built-in integral types; the bool, char, and enum types; and the string type. At the end of each case clause, you must say explicitly where execution is to go next, with some kind of jump statement. Here are the options:

- break (jumps to the end of the switch statement)
- goto case *x* (jumps to another case clause)
- goto default (jumps to the default clause)
- Any other jump statement—namely, return, throw, con tinue, or goto *label*

When more than one value should execute the same code, you can list the common cases sequentially:

```
switch (cardNumber)
{
  case 13:
  case 12:
  case 11:
    Console.WriteLine ("Face card");
    break;
  default:
    Console.WriteLine ("Plain card");
    break;
}
```

This feature of a switch statement can be pivotal in terms of producing cleaner code than multiple if-else statements.

The switch statement with patterns

From C# 7, you can switch on *type*:

```
static void TellMeTheType (object x)
{
  switch (x)
  {
```

```
      case int i:
        Console.WriteLine ("It's an int!");
        break;
      case string s:
        Console.WriteLine (s.Length);      // We can use s
        break;
      case bool b when b == true:   // Fires when b is true
        Console.WriteLine ("True");
        break;
      case null:      // You can also switch on null
        Console.WriteLine ("null");
        break;
    }
  }
```

(The object type allows for a variable of any type—see "Inheritance" on page 83 and "The object Type" on page 91.)

Each *case* clause specifies a type upon which to match, and a variable upon which to assign the typed value if the match succeeds. Unlike with constants, there's no restriction on what types you can use. The optional when clause specifies a condition that must be satisfied for the case to match.

The order of the case clauses is relevant when you're switching on type (unlike when you're switching on constants). An exception to this rule is the default clause, which is executed last, regardless of where it appears.

You can stack multiple case clauses. The Console.WriteLine in the following code will execute for any floating-point type greater than 1,000:

```
switch (x)
{
  case float f when f > 1000:
  case double d when d > 1000:
  case decimal m when m > 1000:
    Console.WriteLine ("f, d and m are out of scope");
    break;
```

In this example, the compiler lets us consume the variables f, d, and m, *only* in the when clauses. When we call Console.Write

---

Line, it's unknown as to which one of those three variables will be assigned, so the compiler puts all of them out of scope.

Switch expressions (C# 8)

From C# 8, you can also use switch in the context of an *expression*. Assuming cardName is of type int, the following illustrates its use:

```
string cardName = cardNumber switch
{
  13 => "King",
  12 => "Queen",
  11 => "Jack",
  _ => "Pip card"   // equivalent to 'default'
};
```

Notice that the switch keyword appears *after* the variable name, and that the case clauses are expressions (terminated by commas) rather than statements. You can also switch on multiple values (*tuples*):

```
int cardNumber = 12; string suite = "spades";
string cardName = (cardNumber, suite) switch
{
  (13, "spades") => "King of spades",
  (13, "clubs") => "King of clubs",
  ...
};
```

Iteration Statements

C# enables a sequence of statements to execute repeatedly with the while, do-while, for, and foreach statements.

while and do-while loops

while loops repeatedly execute a body of code while a bool expression is true. The expression is tested *before* the body of the loop is executed. For example, the following writes 012:

```
int i = 0;
while (i < 3)
{                              // Braces here are optional
  Console.Write (i++);
}
```

do-while loops differ in functionality from while loops only in that they test the expression *after* the statement block has executed (ensuring that the block is always executed at least once). Here's the preceding example rewritten with a do-while loop:

```
int i = 0;
do
{
  Console.WriteLine (i++);
}
while (i < 3);
```

for loops

for loops are like while loops with special clauses for *initialization* and *iteration* of a loop variable. A for loop contains three clauses as follows:

```
for (init-clause; condition-clause; iteration-clause)
    statement-or-statement-block
```

The *init-clause* executes before the loop begins, and typically initializes one or more *iteration* variables.

The *condition-clause* is a bool expression that is tested *before* each loop iteration. The body executes while this condition is true.

The *iteration-clause* is executed *after* each iteration of the body. It's typically used to update the iteration variable.

For example, the following prints the numbers 0 through 2:

```
for (int i = 0; i < 3; i++)
    Console.WriteLine (i);
```

The following prints the first 10 Fibonacci numbers (where each number is the sum of the previous two):

```
for (int i = 0, prevFib = 1, curFib = 1; i < 10; i++)
{
  Console.WriteLine (prevFib);
  int newFib = prevFib + curFib;
  prevFib = curFib; curFib = newFib;
}
```

Any of the three parts of the for statement can be omitted. You can implement an infinite loop such as the following (though while(true) can be used, instead):

```
for (;;) Console.WriteLine ("interrupt me");
```

foreach loops

The foreach statement iterates over each element in an enumerable object. Most of the types in C# and .NET Core that represent a set or list of elements are enumerable. For example, both an array and a string are enumerable. Here is an example of enumerating over the characters in a string, from the first character through to the last:

```
foreach (char c in "beer")
  Console.WriteLine (c + " ");    // b e e r
```

We define enumerable objects in "Enumeration and Iterators" on page 144.

Jump Statements

The C# jump statements are break, continue, goto, return, and throw. We cover the throw keyword in "try Statements and Exceptions" on page 135.

The break statement

The break statement ends the execution of the body of an iteration or switch statement:

```
int x = 0;
while (true)
{
  if (x++ > 5) break;     // break from the loop
}
```

```
// execution continues here after break
...
```

The continue statement

The continue statement forgoes the remaining statements in the loop and makes an early start on the next iteration. The following loop *skips* even numbers:

```
for (int i = 0; i < 10; i++)
{
  if ((i % 2) == 0) continue;
  Console.Write (i + " ");      // 1 3 5 7 9
}
```

The goto statement

The goto statement transfers execution to a label (denoted with a colon suffix) within a statement block. The following iterates the numbers 1 through 5, mimicking a for loop:

```
int i = 1;
startLoop:
if (i <= 5)
{
  Console.Write (i + " ");   // 1 2 3 4 5
  i++;
  goto startLoop;
}
```

The return statement

The return statement exits the method and must return an expression of the method's return type if the method is nonvoid:

```
static decimal AsPercentage (decimal d)
{
  decimal p = d * 100m;
  return p;    // Return to calling method with value
}
```

A return statement can appear anywhere in a method (except in a finally block) and can be used more than once.

Namespaces

A namespace is a domain within which type names must be unique. Types are typically organized into hierarchical namespaces—both to avoid naming conflicts and to make type names easier to find. For example, the RSA type that handles public key encryption is defined within the following namespace:

```
System.Security.Cryptography
```

A namespace forms an integral part of a type's name. The following code calls RSA's Create method:

```
System.Security.Cryptography.RSA rsa =
  System.Security.Cryptography.RSA.Create();
```

NOTE

Namespaces are independent of assemblies, which are units of deployment such as an *.exe* or *.dll*.

Namespaces also have no impact on member accessibility—public, internal, private, and so on.

The namespace keyword defines a namespace for types within that block. For example:

```
namespace Outer.Middle.Inner
{
  class Class1 {}
  class Class2 {}
}
```

The dots in the namespace indicate a hierarchy of nested namespaces. The code that follows is semantically identical to the preceding example:

```
namespace Outer
{
  namespace Middle
  {
```

```
    namespace Inner
    {
      class Class1 {}
      class Class2 {}
    }
  }
}
```

You can refer to a type with its *fully qualified name*, which includes all namespaces from the outermost to the innermost. For example, you could refer to Class1 in the preceding example as Outer.Middle.Inner.Class1.

Types not defined in any namespace are said to reside in the *global namespace*. The global namespace also includes top-level namespaces, such as Outer in our example.

The using Directive

The using directive *imports* a namespace and is a convenient way to refer to types without their fully qualified names. For example, you can refer to Class1 in the preceding example as follows:

```
using Outer.Middle.Inner;

class Test      // Test is in the global namespace
{
  static void Main()
  {
    Class1 c;    // Don't need fully qualified name
    ...
  }
}
```

A using directive can be nested within a namespace itself to limit the scope of the directive.

using static

From C# 6, you can import not just a namespace, but a specific type, with the using static directive. All static members of that type can then be used without being qualified with the type name. In the following example, we call the `Console` class's static `WriteLine` method:

```
using static System.Console;

class Test
{
  static void Main() { WriteLine ("Hello"); }
}
```

The `using static` directive imports all accessible static members of the type, including fields, properties, and nested types. You can also apply this directive to enum types (see "Enums" on page 104), in which case their members are imported. Should an ambiguity arise between multiple static imports, the C# compiler is unable to infer the correct type from the context, and will generate an error.

Rules Within a Namespace

Name scoping

Names declared in outer namespaces can be used unqualified within inner namespaces. In this example, `Class1` does not need qualification within `Inner`:

```
namespace Outer
{
  class Class1 {}

  namespace Inner
  {
    class Class2 : Class1 {}
  }
}
```

If you want to refer to a type in a different branch of your namespace hierarchy, you can use a partially qualified name. In the following example, we base `SalesReport` on `Common.Report Base`:

```
namespace MyTradingCompany
{
  namespace Common
  {
    class ReportBase {}
  }
  namespace ManagementReporting
  {
    class SalesReport : Common.ReportBase {}
  }
}
```

Name hiding

If the same type name appears in both an inner and an outer
namespace, the inner name wins. To refer to the type in the
outer namespace, you must qualify its name.

NOTE

All type names are converted to fully qualified names at
compile time. Intermediate Language (IL) code contains
no unqualified or partially qualified names.

Repeated namespaces

You can repeat a namespace declaration, as long as the type
names within the namespaces don't conflict:

```
namespace Outer.Middle.Inner { class Class1 {} }
namespace Outer.Middle.Inner { class Class2 {} }
```

The classes can even span source files and assemblies.

The global:: qualifier

Occasionally, a fully qualified type name might conflict with an
inner name. You can force C# to use the fully qualified type
name by prefixing it with global::, as follows:

```
global::System.Text.StringBuilder sb;
```

Aliasing Types and Namespaces

Importing a namespace can result in type-name collision.
Rather than importing the whole namespace, you can import
just the specific types you need, giving each type an alias. For
example:

```
using PropertyInfo2 = System.Reflection.PropertyInfo;
class Program { PropertyInfo2 p; }
```

An entire namespace can be aliased, as follows:

```
using R = System.Reflection;
class Program { R.PropertyInfo p; }
```

Classes

A class is the most common kind of reference type. The simplest possible class declaration is as follows:

```
class Foo
{
}
```

A more complex class optionally has the following:

Preceding the keyword class	*Attributes* and *class modifiers*. The non-nested class modifiers are public, internal, abstract, sealed, static, unsafe, and partial.
Following Foo	*Generic type parameters* and *constraints*, a *base class*, and *interfaces*.
Within the braces	*Class members* (these are *methods*, *properties*, *indexers*, *events*, *fields*, *constructors*, *overloaded operators*, *nested types*, and a *finalizer*).

Fields

A *field* is a variable that is a member of a class or struct. For
example:

```
class Octopus
{
  string name;
```

```
    public int Age = 10;
}
```

A field can have the `readonly` modifier to prevent it from being modified after construction. A read-only field can be assigned only in its declaration or within the enclosing type's constructor.

Field initialization is optional. An uninitialized field has a default value (0, \0, null, false). Field initializers run before constructors in the order in which they appear.

For convenience, you can declare multiple fields of the same type in a comma-separated list. This is a convenient way for all the fields to share the same attributes and field modifiers. For example:

```
static readonly int legs = 8, eyes = 2;
```

Constants

A *constant* is evaluated statically at compile time and the compiler literally substitutes its value whenever used (rather like a macro in C++). A constant can be any of the built-in numeric types: bool, char, string, or an enum type.

A constant is declared with the `const` keyword and must be initialized with a value. For example:

```
public class Test
{
  public const string Message = "Hello World";
}
```

A constant is much more restrictive than a `static readonly` field—both in the types you can use and in field initialization semantics. A constant also differs from a `static readonly` field in that the evaluation of the constant occurs at compile time. Constants can also be declared local to a method:

```
static void Main()
{
  const double twoPI = 2 * System.Math.PI;
```

```
    ...
}
```

Methods

A method performs an action in a series of statements. A method can receive *input* data from the caller by specifying *parameters*, and *output* data back to the caller by specifying a *return type*. A method can specify a void return type, indicating that it doesn't return any value to its caller. A method can also output data back to the caller via ref and out parameters.

A method's *signature* must be unique within the type. A method's signature comprises its name and parameter types in order (but not the parameter *names*, nor the return type).

Expression-bodied methods

A method that comprises a single expression, such as the following:

```
int Foo (int x) { return x * 2; }
```

can be written more tersely as an *expression-bodied method* (from C# 6). A fat arrow replaces the braces and return keyword:

```
int Foo (int x) => x * 2;
```

Expression-bodied functions can also have a void return type:

```
void Foo (int x) => Console.WriteLine (x);
```

Overloading methods

A type can overload methods (have multiple methods with the same name), as long as the parameter types are different. For example, the following methods can all coexist in the same type:

```
void Foo (int x);
void Foo (double x);
void Foo (int x, float y);
void Foo (float x, int y);
```

Local methods

From C# 7, you can define a method within another method:

```csharp
void WriteCubes()
{
  Console.WriteLine (Cube (3));

  int Cube (int value) => value * value * value;
}
```

The local method (Cube, in this case) is visible only to the enclosing method (WriteCubes). This simplifies the containing type and instantly signals to anyone looking at the code that Cube is used nowhere else. Local methods can access the local variables and parameters of the enclosing method. This has a number of consequences, which we describe in "Capturing Outer Variables" on page 131.

Local methods can appear within other function kinds, such as property accessors, constructors, and so on, and even within other local methods. Local methods can be iterators or asynchronous.

Static local methods (C# 8)

Adding the static modifier to a local method prevents it from seeing the local variables and parameters of the enclosing method. This helps to reduce coupling as well as enabling the local method to declare variables as it pleases, without risk of colliding with those in the containing method.

Instance Constructors

Constructors run initialization code on a class or struct. A constructor is defined like a method, except that the method name and return type are reduced to the name of the enclosing type:

```
public class Panda
{
  string name;                // Define field
  public Panda (string n)     // Define constructor
  {
    name = n;                 // Initialization code
  }
}
...
Panda p = new Panda ("Petey");   // Call constructor
```

From C# 7, single-statement constructors can be written as expression-bodied members:

```
public Panda (string n) => name = n;
```

A class or struct can overload constructors. One overload can call another, using the this keyword:

```
public class Wine
{
  public Wine (decimal price) {...}

  public Wine (decimal price, int year)
                : this (price) {...}
}
```

When one constructor calls another, the *called constructor* executes first.

You can pass an *expression* into another constructor as follows:

```
public Wine (decimal price, DateTime year)
              : this (price, year.Year) {...}
```

The expression itself cannot make use of the this reference, for example, to call an instance method. It can, however, call static methods.

Implicit parameterless constructors

For classes, the C# compiler automatically generates a parameterless public constructor if and only if you do not define any constructors. However, as soon as you define at least one constructor, the parameterless constructor is no longer automatically generated.

Nonpublic constructors

Constructors do not need to be public. A common reason to have a nonpublic constructor is to control instance creation via a static method call. The static method could be used to return an object from a pool rather than creating a new object or to return a specialized subclass chosen based on input arguments.

Deconstructors

Whereas a constructor typically takes a set of values (as parameters) and assigns them to fields, a deconstructor (C# 7+) does the reverse and assigns fields back to a set of variables. A deconstruction method must be called `Deconstruct` and have one or more out parameters:

```
class Rectangle
{
  public readonly float Width, Height;

  public Rectangle (float width, float height)
  {
    Width = width; Height = height;
  }

  public void Deconstruct (out float width,
                           out float height)
  {
    width = Width; height = Height;
  }
}
```

To call the deconstructor, you use the following special syntax:

```
var rect = new Rectangle (3, 4);
(float width, float height) = rect;
Console.WriteLine (width + " " + height);    // 3 4
```

The second line is the deconstructing call. It creates two local variables and then calls the `Deconstruct` method. Our deconstructing call is equivalent to the following:

```
rect.Deconstruct (out var width, out var height);
```

Deconstructing calls allow implicit typing, so we could shorten our call to:

```
(var width, var height) = rect;
```

Or simply:

```
var (width, height) = rect;
```

If the variables into which you're deconstructing are already defined, omit the types altogether; this is called a *deconstructing assignment*:

```
(width, height) = rect;
```

You can offer the caller a range of deconstruction options by overloading the Deconstruct method.

NOTE

The Deconstruct method can be an extension method (see "Extension Methods" on page 156). This is a useful trick, if you want to deconstruct types that you did not author.

Object Initializers

To simplify object initialization, the accessible fields or properties of an object can be initialized via an *object initializer* directly after construction. For example, consider the following class:

```
public class Bunny
{
  public string Name;
  public bool LikesCarrots, LikesHumans;

  public Bunny () {}
  public Bunny (string n) { Name = n; }
}
```

Using object initializers, you can instantiate Bunny objects as follows:

```
Bunny b1 = new Bunny {
                        Name="Bo",
                        LikesCarrots = true,
                        LikesHumans = false
                     };

Bunny b2 = new Bunny ("Bo") {
                              LikesCarrots = true,
                              LikesHumans = false
                            };
```

The this Reference

The this reference refers to the instance itself. In the following example, the Marry method uses this to set the partner's mate field:

```
public class Panda
{
  public Panda Mate;

  public void Marry (Panda partner)
  {
    Mate = partner;
    partner.Mate = this;
  }
}
```

The this reference also disambiguates a local variable or parameter from a field. For example:

```
public class Test
{
  string name;
  public Test (string name) { this.name = name; }
}
```

The this reference is valid only within nonstatic members of a class or struct.

Properties

Properties look like fields from the outside, but internally they contain logic, like methods do. For example, you can't determine by looking at the following code whether `CurrentPrice` is a field or a property:

```
Stock msft = new Stock();
msft.CurrentPrice = 30;
msft.CurrentPrice -= 3;
Console.WriteLine (msft.CurrentPrice);
```

A property is declared like a field, but with a get/set block added. Here's how to implement `CurrentPrice` as a property:

```
public class Stock
{
  decimal currentPrice;  // The private "backing" field

  public decimal CurrentPrice     // The public property
  {
    get { return currentPrice; }
    set { currentPrice = value; }
  }
}
```

get and set denote property *accessors*. The get accessor runs when the property is read. It must return a value of the property's type. The set accessor runs when the property is assigned. It has an implicit parameter named `value` of the property's type that you typically assign to a private field (in this case, `current Price`).

Although properties are accessed in the same way as fields, they differ in that they give the implementer complete control over getting and setting its value. This control enables the implementer to choose whatever internal representation is needed, without exposing the internal details to the user of the property. In this example, the set method could throw an exception if `value` was outside a valid range of values.

Throughout this book, we use public fields to keep the examples free of distraction. In a real application, you would typically favor public properties over public fields to promote encapsulation.

A property is read-only if it specifies only a get accessor, and it is write-only if it specifies only a set accessor. Write-only properties are rarely used.

A property typically has a dedicated backing field to store the underlying data. However, it doesn't need to; it can instead return a value computed from other data.

```
decimal currentPrice, sharesOwned;

public decimal Worth
{
  get { return currentPrice * sharesOwned; }
}
```

Expression-bodied properties

From C# 6, you can declare a read-only property, such as the preceding one, more tersely as an *expression-bodied property*. A fat arrow replaces all the braces and the get and return keywords:

```
public decimal Worth => currentPrice * sharesOwned;
```

From C# 7, set accessors can be expression-bodied, too:

```
public decimal Worth
{
  get => currentPrice * sharesOwned;
  set => sharesOwned = value / currentPrice;
}
```

Automatic properties

The most common implementation for a property is a getter and/or setter that simply reads and writes to a private field of the same type as the property. An *automatic property* declaration instructs the compiler to provide this implementation. We can improve the first example in this section by declaring CurrentPrice as an automatic property:

```
public class Stock
{
  public decimal CurrentPrice { get; set; }
}
```

The compiler automatically generates a private backing field of a compiler-generated name that cannot be referred to. The set accessor can be marked private or protected if you want to expose the property as read-only to other types.

Property initializers

From C# 6, you can add a *property initializer* to automatic properties, just as with fields:

```
public decimal CurrentPrice { get; set; } = 123;
```

This gives CurrentPrice an initial value of 123. Properties with an initializer can be read-only:

```
public int Maximum { get; } = 999;
```

Just as with read-only fields, read-only automatic properties can also be assigned in the type's constructor. This is useful in creating *immutable* (read-only) types.

get and set accessibility

The get and set accessors can have different access levels. The typical use case for this is to have a public property with an internal or private access modifier on the setter:

```
private decimal x;
public decimal X
{
  get        { return x;  }
  private set { x = Math.Round (value, 2); }
}
```

Notice that you declare the property itself with the more permissive access level (public, in this case), and add the modifier to the accessor you want to be *less* accessible.

Indexers

Indexers provide a natural syntax for accessing elements in a class or struct that encapsulate a list or dictionary of values. Indexers are similar to properties, but are accessed via an index argument rather than a property name. The string class has an indexer that lets you access each of its char values via an int index:

```
string s = "hello";
Console.WriteLine (s[0]); // 'h'
Console.WriteLine (s[3]); // 'l'
```

The syntax for using indexers is like that for using arrays, except that the index argument(s) can be of any type(s). You can call indexers null-conditionally by inserting a question mark before the square bracket (see "Null Operators" on page 51):

```
string s = null;
Console.WriteLine (s?[0]);  // Writes nothing; no error.
```

Implementing an indexer

To write an indexer, define a property called this, specifying the arguments in square brackets. For example:

```
class Sentence
{
  string[] words = "The quick brown fox".Split();

  public string this [int wordNum]        // indexer
  {
    get { return words [wordNum];  }
    set { words [wordNum] = value; }
  }
}
```

Here's how we could use this indexer:

```
Sentence s = new Sentence();
Console.WriteLine (s[3]);        // fox
s[3] = "kangaroo";
Console.WriteLine (s[3]);        // kangaroo
```

A type can declare multiple indexers, each with parameters of different types. An indexer can also take more than one parameter:

```
public string this [int arg1, string arg2]
{
  get { ... }  set { ... }
}
```

If you omit the set accessor, an indexer becomes read-only, and expression-bodied syntax can be used (from C# 6) to shorten its definition:

```
public string this [int wordNum] => words [wordNum];
```

Using indices and ranges with indexers (C# 8)

You can support indices and ranges (see "Indices and Ranges (C# 8)" on page 33) in your own classes by defining an indexer with a parameter type of Index or Range. We could extend our previous example, by adding the following indexers to the Sentence class:

```
public string this [Index index] => words [index];
public string[] this [Range range] => words [range];
```

This then enables the following:

```
Sentence s = new Sentence();
Console.WriteLine (s [^1]);        // fox
string[] firstTwoWords = s [..2];  // (The, quick)
```

Static Constructors

A static constructor executes once per *type*, rather than once per *instance*. A type can define only one static constructor, and it must be parameterless and have the same name as the type:

```
class Test
{
```

```
    static Test() { Console.Write ("Type Initialized"); }
}
```

The runtime automatically invokes a static constructor just prior to the type being used. Two things trigger this: instantiating the type, and accessing a static member in the type.

NOTE

If a static constructor throws an unhandled exception, that type becomes *unusable* for the life of the application.

Static field initializers run just *before* the static constructor is called. If a type has no static constructor, static field initializers will execute just prior to the type being used—or *anytime earlier* at the whim of the runtime.

Static Classes

A class can be marked static, indicating that it must be composed solely of static members and cannot be subclassed. The System.Console and System.Math classes are good examples of static classes.

Finalizers

Finalizers are class-only methods that execute before the garbage collector reclaims the memory for an unreferenced object. The syntax for a finalizer is the name of the class prefixed with the ~ symbol:

```
class Class1
{
  ~Class1() { ... }
}
```

C# translates a finalizer into a method that overrides the Final ize method in the object class. We discuss garbage collection and finalizers fully in Chapter 12 of *C# 8.0 in a Nutshell*.

From C# 7, single-statement finalizers can be written with expression-bodied syntax.

Partial Types and Methods

Partial types allow a type definition to be split—typically across multiple files. A common scenario is for a partial class to be autogenerated from some other source (e.g., a Visual Studio template), and for that class to be augmented with additional hand-authored methods. For example:

```
// PaymentFormGen.cs - autogenerated
partial class PaymentForm { ... }

// PaymentForm.cs - hand-authored
partial class PaymentForm { ... }
```

Each participant must have the `partial` declaration.

Participants cannot have conflicting members. A constructor with the same parameters, for instance, cannot be repeated. Partial types are resolved entirely by the compiler, which means that each participant must be available at compile time and must reside in the same assembly.

A base class can be specified on a single participant or on multiple participants (as long as the base class that you specify is the same). In addition, each participant can independently specify interfaces to implement. We cover base classes and interfaces in "Inheritance" on page 83 and "Interfaces" on page 100.

Partial methods

A partial type can contain *partial methods*. These let an autogenerated partial type provide customizable hooks for manual authoring. For example:

```
partial class PaymentForm    // In autogenerated file
{
  partial void ValidatePayment (decimal amount);
}
```

```
partial class PaymentForm      // In hand-authored file
{
  partial void ValidatePayment (decimal amount)
  {
    if (amount > 100) Console.Write ("Expensive!");
  }
}
```

A partial method consists of two parts: a *definition* and an *implementation*. The definition is typically written by a code generator, and the implementation is typically manually authored. If an implementation is not provided, the definition of the partial method is compiled away (as is the code that calls it). This allows autogenerated code to be liberal in providing hooks, without having to worry about bloat. Partial methods must be void and are implicitly private.

The nameof Operator

The nameof operator (introduced in C# 6) returns the name of any symbol (type, member, variable, and so on) as a string:

```
int count = 123;
string name = nameof (count);      // name is "count"
```

Its advantage over simply specifying a string is that of static type checking. Tools such as Visual Studio can understand the symbol reference, so if you rename the symbol in question, all of its references will be renamed, too.

To specify the name of a type member such as a field or property, include the type as well. This works with both static and instance members:

```
string name = nameof (StringBuilder.Length);
```

This evaluates to "Length". To return "StringBuilder.Length", you would do this:

```
nameof(StringBuilder)+"."+nameof(StringBuilder.Length);
```

Inheritance

A class can *inherit* from another class to extend or customize the original class. Inheriting from a class lets you reuse the functionality in that class instead of building it from scratch. A class can inherit from only a single class, but can itself be inherited by many classes, thus forming a class hierarchy. In this example, we begin by defining a class called Asset:

```
public class Asset { public string Name; }
```

Next, we define classes called Stock and House, which will inherit from Asset. Stock and House get everything an Asset has, plus any additional members that they define:

```
public class Stock : Asset   // inherits from Asset
{
  public long SharesOwned;
}

public class House : Asset   // inherits from Asset
{
  public decimal Mortgage;
}
```

Here's how we can use these classes:

```
Stock msft = new Stock { Name="MSFT",
                         SharesOwned=1000 };

Console.WriteLine (msft.Name);        // MSFT
Console.WriteLine (msft.SharesOwned); // 1000

House mansion = new House { Name="Mansion",
                            Mortgage=250000 };

Console.WriteLine (mansion.Name);     // Mansion
Console.WriteLine (mansion.Mortgage); // 250000
```

The *subclasses*, Stock and House, inherit the Name property from the *base class*, Asset.

Subclasses are also called *derived classes*.

Polymorphism

References are polymorphic. This means a variable of type x can refer to an object that subclasses x. For instance, consider the following method:

```
public static void Display (Asset asset)
{
  System.Console.WriteLine (asset.Name);
}
```

This method can display both a Stock and a House because they are both Assets. Polymorphism works on the basis that subclasses (Stock and House) have all the features of their base class (Asset). The converse, however, is not true. If Display were rewritten to accept a House, you could not pass in an Asset.

Casting and Reference Conversions

An object reference can be:

- Implicitly *upcast* to a base class reference
- Explicitly *downcast* to a subclass reference

Upcasting and downcasting between compatible reference types performs *reference conversions*: a new reference is created that points to the *same* object. An upcast always succeeds; a downcast succeeds only if the object is suitably typed.

Upcasting

An upcast operation creates a base class reference from a subclass reference. For example:

```
Stock msft = new Stock();    // From previous example
Asset a = msft;              // Upcast
```

After the upcast, variable a still references the same Stock object as variable msft. The object being referenced is not itself altered or converted:

```
Console.WriteLine (a == msft);       // True
```

Although a and msft refer to the same object, a has a more restrictive view on that object:

```
Console.WriteLine (a.Name);          // OK
Console.WriteLine (a.SharesOwned);   // Compile-time
error
```

The last line generates a compile-time error because the variable a is of type Asset, even though it refers to an object of type Stock. To get to its SharesOwned field, you must *downcast* the Asset to a Stock.

Downcasting

A downcast operation creates a subclass reference from a base class reference. For example:

```
Stock msft = new Stock();
Asset a = msft;                        // Upcast
Stock s = (Stock)a;                    // Downcast
Console.WriteLine (s.SharesOwned);     // <No error>
Console.WriteLine (s == a);            // True
Console.WriteLine (s == msft);         // True
```

As with an upcast, only references are affected—not the underlying object. A downcast requires an explicit cast because it can potentially fail at runtime:

```
House h = new House();
Asset a = h;            // Upcast always succeeds
Stock s = (Stock)a;     // Downcast fails: a is not a Stock
```

If a downcast fails, an InvalidCastException is thrown. This is an example of *runtime type checking* (see "Static and Runtime Type Checking" on page 93).

The as operator

The as operator performs a downcast that evaluates to null (rather than throwing an exception) if the downcast fails:

```
Asset a = new Asset();
Stock s = a as Stock;   // s is null; no exception thrown
```

This is useful when you're going to subsequently test whether the result is null:

```
if (s != null) Console.WriteLine (s.SharesOwned);
```

The as operator cannot perform *custom conversions* (see "Operator Overloading" on page 196) and it cannot do numeric conversions.

The is operator

The is operator tests whether a reference conversion would succeed—in other words, whether an object derives from a specified class (or implements an interface). It is often used to test before downcasting:

```
if (a is Stock) Console.Write (((Stock)a).SharesOwned);
```

The is operator also evaluates to true if an unboxing conversion would succeed (see "The object Type" on page 91). However, it does not consider custom or numeric conversions.

From C# 7, you can introduce a variable while using the is operator:

```
if (a is Stock s)
  Console.WriteLine (s.SharesOwned);
```

The variable that you introduce is available for "immediate" consumption, and remains in scope outside the is expression:

```
if (a is Stock s && s.SharesOwned > 100000)
  Console.WriteLine ("Wealthy");
else
  s = new Stock();   // s is in scope

Console.WriteLine (s.SharesOwned);  // Still in scope
```

Virtual Function Members

A function marked as virtual can be *overridden* by subclasses wanting to provide a specialized implementation. Methods, properties, indexers, and events can all be declared virtual:

```
public class Asset
{
  public string Name;
  public virtual decimal Liability => 0;
}
```

(Liability => 0 is a shortcut for { get { return 0; } }. See
"Expression-bodied properties" on page 76 for more details on
this syntax.) A subclass overrides a virtual method by applying
the override modifier:

```
public class House : Asset
{
  public decimal Mortgage;

  public override decimal Liability => Mortgage;
}
```

By default, the Liability of an Asset is 0. A Stock does not
need to specialize this behavior. However, the House specializes
the Liability property to return the value of the Mortgage:

```
House mansion = new House { Name="Mansion",
                            Mortgage=250000 };
Asset a = mansion;
Console.WriteLine (mansion.Liability);  // 250000
Console.WriteLine (a.Liability);        // 250000
```

The signatures, return types, and accessibility of the virtual and
overridden methods must be identical. An overridden method
can call its base class implementation via the base keyword (see
"The base Keyword" on page 89).

Abstract Classes and Abstract Members

A class declared as *abstract* can never be instantiated. Instead,
only its concrete *subclasses* can be instantiated.

Abstract classes are able to define *abstract members*. Abstract
members are like virtual members, except they don't provide a
default implementation. That implementation must be provided by the subclass, unless that subclass is also declared
abstract:

```
public abstract class Asset
{
  // Note empty implementation
  public abstract decimal NetValue { get; }
}
```

Subclasses override abstract members just as though they were virtual.

Hiding Inherited Members

A base class and a subclass can define identical members. For example:

```
public class A      { public int Counter = 1; }
public class B : A  { public int Counter = 2; }
```

The Counter field in class B is said to *hide* the Counter field in class A. Usually, this happens by accident, when a member is added to the base type *after* an identical member was added to the subtype. For this reason, the compiler generates a warning, and then resolves the ambiguity as follows:

- References to A (at compile time) bind to A.Counter.

- References to B (at compile time) bind to B.Counter.

Occasionally, you want to hide a member deliberately, in which case you can apply the new modifier to the member in the subclass. The new modifier *does nothing more than suppress the compiler warning that would otherwise result*:

```
public class A      { public    int Counter = 1; }
public class B : A  { public new int Counter = 2; }
```

The new modifier communicates your intent to the compiler—and other programmers—that the duplicate member is not an accident.

Sealing Functions and Classes

An overridden function member can *seal* its implementation with the sealed keyword to prevent it from being overridden by further subclasses. In our earlier virtual function member example, we could have sealed House's implementation of Lia bility, preventing a class that derives from House from overriding Liability, as follows:

```
public sealed override decimal Liability { get { ... } }
```

You can also seal the class itself, implicitly sealing all the virtual functions, by applying the sealed modifier to the class itself.

The base Keyword

The base keyword is similar to the this keyword. It serves two essential purposes: accessing an overridden function member from the subclass, and calling a base class constructor (see the next section).

In this example, House uses the base keyword to access Asset's implementation of Liability:

```
public class House : Asset
{
  ...
  public override decimal Liability
    => base.Liability + Mortgage;
}
```

With the base keyword, we access Asset's Liability property *nonvirtually*. This means that we will always access Asset's version of this property, regardless of the instance's actual runtime type.

The same approach works if Liability is *hidden* rather than *overridden*. (You can also access hidden members by casting to the base class before invoking the function.)

Constructors and Inheritance

A subclass must declare its own constructors. For example, if we define Baseclass and Subclass as

```
public class Baseclass
{
  public int X;
```

```
   public Baseclass () { }
   public Baseclass (int x) { this.X = x; }
}
public class Subclass : Baseclass { }
```

the following is illegal:

```
Subclass s = new Subclass (123);
```

Subclass must "redefine" any constructors that it wants to expose. In doing so, it can call any of the base class's constructors with the base keyword:

```
public class Subclass : Baseclass
{
   public Subclass (int x) : base (x) { ... }
}
```

The base keyword works rather like the this keyword, except that it calls a constructor in the base class. Base class constructors always execute first; this ensures that *base* initialization occurs before *specialized* initialization.

If a constructor in a subclass omits the base keyword, the base type's *parameterless* constructor is implicitly called (if the base class has no accessible parameterless constructor, the compiler generates an error).

Constructor and field initialization order

When an object is instantiated, initialization takes place in the following order:

1. From subclass to base class:

    a. Fields are initialized.

    b. Arguments to base class constructor calls are evaluated.

2. From base class to subclass:

    a. Constructor bodies execute.

Overloading and Resolution

Inheritance has an interesting impact on method overloading. Consider the following two overloads:

```
static void Foo (Asset a) { }
static void Foo (House h) { }
```

When an overload is called, the most specific type has precedence:

```
House h = new House (...);
Foo(h);                    // Calls Foo(House)
```

The particular overload to call is determined statically (at compile time) rather than at runtime. The following code calls Foo(Asset), even though the runtime type of a is House:

```
Asset a = new House (...);
Foo(a);                    // Calls Foo(Asset)
```

NOTE

If you cast Asset to dynamic (see "Dynamic Binding" on page 187), the decision as to which overload to call is deferred until runtime and is based on the object's actual type.

The object Type

object (System.Object) is the ultimate base class for all types. Any type can be implicitly upcast to object.

To illustrate how this is useful, consider a general-purpose *stack*. A stack is a data structure based on the principle of LIFO —"last in, first out." A stack has two operations: *push* an object on the stack, and *pop* an object off the stack. Here is a simple implementation that can hold up to 10 objects:

```
public class Stack
{
    int position;
```

```
    object[] data = new object[10];
    public void Push (object o) { data[position++] = o; }
    public object Pop() { return data[--position]; }
}
```

Because Stack works with the object type, we can Push and Pop
instances of *any type* to and from the Stack:

```
Stack stack = new Stack();
stack.Push ("sausage");
string s = (string) stack.Pop();    // Downcast
Console.WriteLine (s);              // sausage
```

object is a reference type, by virtue of being a class. Despite
this, value types, such as int, can also be cast to and from
object. To make this possible, the CLR must perform some
special work to bridge the underlying differences between value
and reference types. This process is called *boxing* and *unboxing*.

NOTE

In "Generics" on page 108, we describe how to improve
our Stack class to better handle stacks with same-typed
elements.

Boxing and Unboxing

Boxing is the act of casting a value type instance to a reference
type instance. The reference type can be either the object class
or an interface (see "Interfaces" on page 100). In this example,
we box an int into an object:

```
int x = 9;
object obj = x;             // Box the int
```

Unboxing reverses the operation by casting the object back to
the original value type:

```
int y = (int)obj;          // Unbox the int
```

Unboxing requires an explicit cast. The runtime checks that the
stated value type matches the actual object type, throwing an

---

InvalidCastException if the check fails. For instance, the following throws an exception, because long does not exactly match int:

```
object obj = 9;          // 9 is inferred to be of type int
long x = (long) obj;     // InvalidCastException
```

The following succeeds, however:

```
object obj = 9;
long x = (int) obj;
```

As does this:

```
object obj = 3.5;          // 3.5 inferred to be type double
int x = (int) (double) obj;     // x is now 3
```

In the last example, (double) performs an *unboxing* and then (int) performs a *numeric conversion*.

Boxing *copies* the value type instance into the new object, and unboxing *copies* the contents of the object back into a value type instance:

```
int i = 3;
object boxed = i;
i = 5;
Console.WriteLine (boxed);     // 3
```

Static and Runtime Type Checking

C# checks types both statically (at compile time) and at runtime.

Static type checking enables the compiler to verify the correctness of your program without running it. The following code will fail because the compiler enforces static typing:

```
int x = "5";
```

Runtime type checking is performed by the CLR when you downcast via a reference conversion or unboxing:

```
object y = "5";
int z = (int) y;          // Runtime error, downcast failed
```

Runtime type checking is possible because each object on the heap internally stores a little type token. You can retrieve this token by calling the GetType method of object.

The GetType Method and typeof Operator

All types in C# are represented at runtime with an instance of System.Type. There are two basic ways to get a System.Type object: call GetType on the instance, or use the typeof operator on a type name. GetType is evaluated at runtime; typeof is evaluated statically at compile time.

System.Type has properties for such things as the type's name, assembly, base type, and so on. For example:

```
int x = 3;

Console.Write (x.GetType().Name);            // Int32
Console.Write (typeof(int).Name);            // Int32
Console.Write (x.GetType().FullName);     // System.Int32
Console.Write (x.GetType() == typeof(int));      // True
```

System.Type also has methods that act as a gateway to the runtime's reflection model. For detailed information, see Chapter 19 of *C# 8.0 in a Nutshell*.

Object Member Listing

Her are all the members of object:

```
public extern Type GetType();
public virtual bool Equals (object obj);
public static bool Equals (object objA, object objB);
public static bool ReferenceEquals (object objA,
                                    object objB);
public virtual int GetHashCode();
public virtual string ToString();
protected virtual void Finalize();
protected extern object MemberwiseClone();
```

Equals, ReferenceEquals, and GetHashCode

The Equals method in the object class is similar to the == operator except that Equals is virtual, whereas == is static. The following example illustrates the difference:

```
object x = 3;
object y = 3;
Console.WriteLine (x == y);        // False
Console.WriteLine (x.Equals (y));  // True
```

Because x and y have been cast to the object type, the compiler statically binds to object's == operator, which uses *reference type* semantics to compare two instances. (And because x and y are boxed, they are represented in separate memory locations, and so are unequal.) The virtual Equals method, however, defers to the Int32 type's Equals method, which uses *value type* semantics in comparing two values.

The static object.Equals method simply calls the virtual Equals method on the first argument—after checking that the arguments are not null:

```
object x = null, y = 3;
bool error = x.Equals (y);      // Runtime error!
bool ok = object.Equals (x, y); // OK (false)
```

ReferenceEquals forces a reference type equality comparison (this is occasionally useful on reference types for which the == operator has been overloaded to do otherwise).

GetHashCode emits a hash code suitable for use with hashtable-based dictionaries such as System.Collections.Generic.Dictio nary and System.Collections.Hashtable.

To customize a type's equality semantics, you must at a minimum override Equals and GetHashCode. You would also usually overload the == and != operators. For an example of how to do both, see "Operator Overloading" on page 196.

The ToString Method

The ToString method returns the default textual representation of a type instance. The ToString method is overridden by all built-in types:

```
string s1 = 1.ToString();     // s1 is "1"
string s2 = true.ToString();  // s2 is "True"
```

You can override the ToString method on custom types as follows:

```
public override string ToString() => "Foo";
```

Structs

A *struct* is similar to a class, with the following key differences:

- A struct is a value type, whereas a class is a reference type.
- A struct does not support inheritance (other than implicitly deriving from object, or more precisely, System.ValueType).

A struct can have all the members that a class can, except for a parameterless constructor, field initializers, a finalizer, and virtual or protected members.

A struct is appropriate when value type semantics are desirable. Good examples are numeric types, where it is more natural for assignment to copy a value rather than a reference. Because a struct is a value type, each instance does not require instantiation of an object on the heap (and subsequent collection); this can incur useful savings when you're creating many instances of a type.

As with any value type, a struct can end up on the heap indirectly, either through boxing, or if it appears as a field in a class. If we were to instantiate SomeClass in the following example, field Y would refer to a struct on the heap:

```
struct SomeStruct { public int X;         }
class SomeClass  { public SomeStruct Y; }
```

Similarly, if you were to declare an array of SomeStruct, the instance would reside on the heap (because arrays are reference types), although the entire array would require only a single memory allocation.

From C# 7.2, you can apply the ref modifier to a struct to ensure that it can be used only in ways that will place it on the stack. This enables further compiler optimizations as well as allowing for the Span<T> type (see *https://bit.ly/2LR2ctm*).

Struct Construction Semantics

The construction semantics of a struct are as follows:

- A parameterless constructor that you can't override implicitly exists. This performs a bitwise-zeroing of its fields.

- When you define a struct constructor (with parameters), you must explicitly assign every field.

- You can't have field initializers in a struct.

readonly Structs and Functions

From C# 7.2, you can apply the readonly modifier to a struct to enforce that all fields are readonly; this aids in declaring intent as well as allowing the compiler more optimization freedom:

```
readonly struct Point
{
   public readonly int X, Y;   // X and Y must be readonly
}
```

If you need to apply readonly at a more granular level, C# 8 assists with a new feature whereby you can apply the readonly modifier to a struct's *functions*. This ensures that if the function attempts to modify any field, a compile-time error is generated:

```
struct Point
{
  public int X, Y;
  public readonly void ResetX() => X = 0;  // Error!
}
```

If a readonly function calls a non-readonly function, the compiler generates a warning (and defensively copies the struct to avoid the possibility of a mutation).

Access Modifiers

To promote encapsulation, a type or type member can limit its *accessibility* to other types and other assemblies by adding one of five *access modifiers* to the declaration:

public
  Fully accessible. This is the implicit accessibility for members of an enum or interface.

internal
  Accessible only within the containing assembly or friend assemblies. This is the default accessibility for non-nested types.

private
  Accessible only within the containing type. This is the default accessibility for members of a class or struct.

protected
  Accessible only within the containing type or subclasses.

protected internal
  The *union* of protected and internal accessibility (this is more *permissive* than protected or internal alone in that it makes a member more accessible in two ways).

private protected *(from C# 7.2)*
  The *intersection* of protected and internal accessibility (this is more *restrictive* than protected or internal alone).

In the following example, `Class2` is accessible from outside its assembly; `Class1` is not:

```
class Class1 {}           // Class1 is internal (default)
public class Class2 {}
```

`ClassB` exposes field `x` to other types in the same assembly; `ClassA` does not:

```
class ClassA { int x;         } // x is private
class ClassB { internal int x; }
```

When you're overriding a base class function, accessibility must be identical on the overridden function. The compiler prevents any inconsistent use of access modifiers—for example, a sub-class itself can be less accessible than a base class, but not more.

Friend Assemblies

You can expose `internal` members to other *friend* assemblies by adding the `System.Runtime.CompilerServices.InternalsVi sibleTo` assembly attribute, specifying the name of the friend assembly as follows:

```
[assembly: InternalsVisibleTo ("Friend")]
```

If the friend assembly is signed with a strong name, you must specify its *full* 160-byte public key. You can extract this key via a Language Integrated Query (LINQ)—an interactive example is given in LINQPad's free sample library for *C# 8.0 in a Nut-shell*, under Chapter 3, Access Modifiers.

Accessibility Capping

A type caps the accessibility of its declared members. The most common example of capping is when you have an `internal` type with `public` members. For example:

```
class C { public void Foo() {} }
```

C's (default) `internal` accessibility caps Foo's accessibility, effec-tively making Foo `internal`. A common reason Foo would be marked public is to make for easier refactoring, should C later be changed to public.

Interfaces

An interface is similar to a class, but it provides a specification rather than an implementation for its members (although from C# 8.0, an interface can provide a *default* implementation; see "Default Interface Members (C# 8)" on page 103). An interface is special in the following ways:

- Interface members are *all implicitly abstract*. In contrast, a class can provide both abstract members and concrete members with implementations.

- A class (or struct) can implement *multiple* interfaces. In contrast, a class can inherit from only a *single* class, and a struct cannot inherit at all (aside from deriving from System.ValueType).

An interface declaration is like a class declaration, but it provides no implementation for its members, because all its members are implicitly abstract. These members will be implemented by the classes and structs that implement the interface. An interface can contain only methods, properties, events, and indexers, which noncoincidentally are precisely the members of a class that can be abstract.

Here is a slightly simplified version of the IEnumerator interface, defined in System.Collections:

```
public interface IEnumerator
{
  bool MoveNext();
  object Current { get; }
  void Reset();
}
```

Interface members are always implicitly public and cannot declare an access modifier. Implementing an interface means providing a public implementation for all of its members:

```
internal class Countdown : IEnumerator
{
  int count = 6;
  public bool MoveNext() => count-- > 0 ;
  public object Current  => count;
  public void Reset()    => count = 6;
}
```

You can implicitly cast an object to any interface that it implements:

```
IEnumerator e = new Countdown();
while (e.MoveNext())
  Console.Write (e.Current + " "); // 5 4 3 2 1 0
```

Extending an Interface

Interfaces can derive from other interfaces. For instance:

```
public interface IUndoable            { void Undo(); }
public interface IRedoable : IUndoable { void Redo(); }
```

IRedoable "inherits" all the members of IUndoable.

Explicit Interface Implementation

Implementing multiple interfaces can sometimes result in a collision between member signatures. You can resolve such collisions by *explicitly implementing* an interface member. For example:

```
interface I1 { void Foo(); }
interface I2 { int Foo();  }

public class Widget : I1, I2
{
  public void Foo()  // Implicit implementation
  {
    Console.Write ("Widget's implementation of I1.Foo");
  }

  int I2.Foo()   // Explicit implementation of I2.Foo
  {
    Console.Write ("Widget's implementation of I2.Foo");
    return 42;
```

```
    }
}
```

Because both I1 and I2 have conflicting Foo signatures, Widget explicitly implements I2's Foo method. This lets the two methods coexist in one class. The only way to call an explicitly implemented member is to cast to its interface:

```
Widget w = new Widget();
w.Foo();              // Widget's implementation of I1.Foo
((I1)w).Foo();        // Widget's implementation of I1.Foo
((I2)w).Foo();        // Widget's implementation of I2.Foo
```

Another reason to explicitly implement interface members is to hide members that are highly specialized and distracting to a type's normal use case. For example, a type that implements ISerializable would typically want to avoid flaunting its ISerializable members unless explicitly cast to that interface.

Implementing Interface Members Virtually

An implicitly implemented interface member is, by default, sealed. It must be marked virtual or abstract in the base class in order to be overridden: calling the interface member through either the base class or the interface then calls the subclass's implementation.

An explicitly implemented interface member cannot be marked virtual, nor can it be overridden in the usual manner. It can, however, be *reimplemented*.

Reimplementing an Interface in a Subclass

A subclass can *reimplement* any interface member already implemented by a base class. Reimplementation hijacks a member implementation (when called through the interface) and works whether or not the member is virtual in the base class.

In the following example, TextBox implements IUndo.Undo explicitly, and so it cannot be marked as virtual. To "override" it, RichTextBox must reimplement IUndo's Undo method:

```
public interface IUndoable { void Undo(); }

public class TextBox : IUndoable
{
  void IUndoable.Undo()
    => Console.WriteLine ("TextBox.Undo");
}

public class RichTextBox : TextBox, IUndoable
{
  public new void Undo()
    => Console.WriteLine ("RichTextBox.Undo");
}
```

Calling the reimplemented member through the interface calls the subclass's implementation:

```
RichTextBox r = new RichTextBox();
r.Undo();                   // RichTextBox.Undo
((IUndoable)r).Undo();      // RichTextBox.Undo
```

In this case, Undo is implemented explicitly. Implicitly implemented members can also be reimplemented, but the effect is nonpervasive in that calling the member through the base class invokes the base implementation.

Default Interface Members (C# 8)

From C# 8, you can add a default implementation to an interface member, making it optional to implement:

```
interface ILogger
{
  void Log (string text) => Console.WriteLine (text);
}
```

This is advantageous if you wish to add a member to an interface defined in a popular library without breaking (potentially thousands of) implementations.

Default implementations are always explicit, so if a class implementing ILogger fails to define a Log method, the only way to call it is through the interface:

```
class Logger : ILogger { }
...
((ILogger)new Logger()).Log ("message");
```

This prevents a problem of multiple implementation inheritance: if the same default member is added to two interfaces that a class implements, there is never an ambiguity as to which member is called.

Interfaces can also now define static members (including fields), which can be accessed from code inside default implementations:

```
interface ILogger
{
  void Log (string text) =>
    Console.WriteLine (Prefix + text);

  static string Prefix = "";
}
```

Because interface members are implicitly public, you can also access static members from the outside:

```
ILogger.Prefix = "File log: ";
```

You can restrict this by adding an accessibility modifier to the static interface member (such as `private`, `protected`, or `internal`).

Instance fields are (still) prohibited. This is in line with the principle of interfaces, which is to define *behavior*, not *state*.

Enums

An enum is a special value type that lets you specify a group of named numeric constants. For example:

```
public enum BorderSide { Left, Right, Top, Bottom }
```

We can use this enum type as follows:

```
BorderSide topSide = BorderSide.Top;
bool isTop = (topSide == BorderSide.Top);   // true
```

Each enum member has an underlying integral-type value. By default, the underlying values are of type int, and the enum members are assigned the constants 0, 1, 2... (in their declaration order). You may specify an alternative integral type, as follows:

```
public enum BorderSide : byte { Left,Right,Top,Bottom }
```

You may also specify an explicit integer value for each member:

```
public enum BorderSide : byte
  { Left=1, Right=2, Top=10, Bottom=11 }
```

The compiler also lets you explicitly assign *some* of the enum members. The unassigned enum members keep incrementing from the last explicit value. The preceding example is equivalent to:

```
public enum BorderSide : byte
  { Left=1, Right, Top=10, Bottom }
```

Enum Conversions

You can convert an enum instance to and from its underlying integral value with an explicit cast:

```
int i = (int) BorderSide.Left;
BorderSide side = (BorderSide) i;
bool leftOrRight = (int) side <= 2;
```

You can also explicitly cast one enum type to another; the translation then uses the members' underlying integral values.

The numeric literal 0 is treated specially in that it does not require an explicit cast:

```
BorderSide b = 0;    // No cast required
if (b == 0) ...
```

In this particular example, BorderSide has no member with an integer value of 0. This does not generate an error: a limitation of enums is that the compiler and CLR do not prevent the assignment of integrals whose values fall outside the range of members:

```
BorderSide b = (BorderSide) 12345;
Console.WriteLine (b);                // 12345
```

Flags Enums

You can combine enum members. To prevent ambiguities, members of a combinable enum require explicitly assigned values, typically in powers of two. For example:

```
[Flags]
public enum BorderSides
  { None=0, Left=1, Right=2, Top=4, Bottom=8 }
```

By convention, a combinable enum type is given a plural rather than singular name. To work with combined enum values, you use bitwise operators, such as | and &. These operate on the underlying integral values:

```
BorderSides leftRight =
  BorderSides.Left | BorderSides.Right;

if ((leftRight & BorderSides.Left) != 0)
  Console.WriteLine ("Includes Left");   // Includes Left

string formatted = leftRight.ToString(); // "Left, Right"

BorderSides s = BorderSides.Left;
s |= BorderSides.Right;
Console.WriteLine (s == leftRight);      // True
```

The Flags attribute should be applied to combinable enum types; if you fail to do this, calling ToString on an enum instance emits a number rather than a series of names.

For convenience, you can include combination members within an enum declaration itself:

```
[Flags] public enum BorderSides
{
  None=0,
  Left=1, Right=2, Top=4, Bottom=8,
  LeftRight = Left | Right,
  TopBottom = Top  | Bottom,
  All       = LeftRight | TopBottom
}
```

Enum Operators

The operators that work with enums are:

```
=   ==  !=  <   >   <=  >=  +   -   ^   &   |   ~
+=  -=  ++  --  sizeof
```

The bitwise, arithmetic, and comparison operators return the result of processing the underlying integral values. Addition is permitted between an enum and an integral type, but not between two enums.

Nested Types

A *nested type* is declared within the scope of another type. For example:

```
public class TopLevel
{
  public class Nested { }                  // Nested class
  public enum Color { Red, Blue, Tan }  // Nested enum
}
```

A nested type has the following features:

- It can access the enclosing type's private members and everything else the enclosing type can access.
- It can be declared with the full range of access modifiers, rather than just public and internal.
- The default accessibility for a nested type is private rather than internal.
- Accessing a nested type from outside the enclosing type requires qualification with the enclosing type's name (like when you're accessing static members).

For example, to access Color.Red from outside our TopLevel class, you'd need to do this:

```
TopLevel.Color color = TopLevel.Color.Red;
```

All types can be nested; however, only classes and structs can nest.

Generics

C# has two separate mechanisms for writing code that is reusable across different types: *inheritance* and *generics*. Whereas inheritance expresses reusability with a base type, generics express reusability with a "template" that contains "placeholder" types. Generics, when compared to inheritance, can *increase type safety* and *reduce casting and boxing*.

Generic Types

A generic type declares *type parameters*—placeholder types to be filled in by the consumer of the generic type, which supplies the *type arguments*. Here is a generic type, Stack<T>, designed to stack instances of type T. Stack<T> declares a single type parameter T:

```
public class Stack<T>
{
  int position;
  T[] data = new T[100];
  public void Push (T obj) => data[position++] = obj;
  public T Pop()          => data[--position];
}
```

We can use Stack<T> as follows:

```
var stack = new Stack<int>();
stack.Push (5);
stack.Push (10);
int x = stack.Pop();      // x is 10
int y = stack.Pop();      // y is 5
```

`Stack<int>` fills in the type parameter T with the type argument
`int`, implicitly creating a type on the fly (the synthesis occurs at
runtime). `Stack<int>` effectively has the following definition
(substitutions appear in bold, with the class name hashed out
to avoid confusion):

```
public class ###
{
  int position;
  int[] data = new int[100];
  public void Push (int obj) => data[position++] = obj;
  public int Pop()           => data[--position];
}
```

Technically, we say that `Stack<T>` is an *open type*, whereas
`Stack<int>` is a *closed type*. At runtime, all generic type instances are closed—with the placeholder types filled in.

Generic Methods

A generic method declares type parameters within the signature of a method. With generic methods, many fundamental
algorithms can be implemented in a general-purpose way. Here
is a generic method that swaps the contents of two variables of
any type T:

```
static void Swap<T> (ref T a, ref T b)
{
  T temp = a; a = b; b = temp;
}
```

You can use Swap<T> as follows:

```
int x = 5, y = 10;
Swap (ref x, ref y);
```

Generally, there is no need to supply type arguments to a generic method, because the compiler can implicitly infer the type. If there is ambiguity, generic methods can be called with the type arguments as follows:

```
Swap<int> (ref x, ref y);
```

Within a generic *type*, a method is not classed as generic unless it *introduces* type parameters (with the angle bracket syntax). The Pop method in our generic stack merely consumes the type's existing type parameter, T, and is not classed as a generic method.

Methods and types are the only constructs that can introduce type parameters. Properties, indexers, events, fields, constructors, operators, and so on cannot declare type parameters, although they can partake in any type parameters already declared by their enclosing type. In our generic stack example, for instance, we could write an indexer that returns a generic item:

```
public T this [int index] { get { return data[index]; } }
```

Similarly, constructors can partake in existing type parameters, but cannot *introduce* them.

Declaring Type Parameters

Type parameters can be introduced in the declaration of classes, structs, interfaces, delegates (see "Delegates" on page 117), and methods. You can specify multiple type parameters by separating them with commas:

```
class Dictionary<TKey, TValue> {...}
```

To instantiate:

```
var myDict = new Dictionary<int,string>();
```

Generic type names and method names can be overloaded as long as the number of type parameters differs. For example, the following three type names do not conflict:

```
class A {}
class A<T> {}
class A<T1,T2> {}
```

NOTE

By convention, generic types and methods with a *single* type parameter name their parameter T, as long as the intent of the parameter is clear. With *multiple* type parameters, each parameter has a more descriptive name (prefixed by T).

---

typeof and Unbound Generic Types

Open generic types do not exist at runtime: open generic types are closed as part of compilation. However, it is possible for an *unbound* generic type to exist at runtime—purely as a Type object. The only way to specify an unbound generic type in C# is with the typeof operator:

```
class A<T> {}
class A<T1,T2> {}
...

Type a1 = typeof (A<>);   // Unbound type
Type a2 = typeof (A<,>);  // Indicates 2 type args
Console.Write (a2.GetGenericArguments().Count()); // 2
```

You can also use the typeof operator to specify a closed type

```
Type a3 = typeof (A<int,int>);
```

or an open type (which is closed at runtime):

```
class B<T> { void X() { Type t = typeof (T); } }
```

The default Generic Value

You can use the `default` keyword to get the default value for a generic type parameter. The default value for a reference type is `null`, and the default value for a value type is the result of bitwise-zeroing the type's fields:

```
static void Zap<T> (T[] array)
{
  for (int i = 0; i < array.Length; i++)
    array[i] = default(T);
}
```

From C# 7.1, you can omit the type argument for cases in which the compiler is able to infer it:

```
array[i] = default;
```

Generic Constraints

By default, a type parameter can be substituted with any type whatsoever. *Constraints* can be applied to a type parameter to require more specific type arguments. There are eight kinds of constraints:

```
where T : base-class  // Base class constraint
where T : interface   // Interface constraint
where T : class       // Reference type constraint
where T : class?      // (See "Nullable Reference Types")
where T : struct      // Value type constraint
where T : unmanaged   // Unmanaged constraint
where T : new()       // Parameterless constructor
                      // constraint
where U : T           // Naked type constraint
```

In the next example, `GenericClass<T,U>` requires `T` to derive from (or be identical to) `SomeClass` and implement `Interface1`, and requires `U` to provide a parameterless constructor:

```
class       SomeClass {}
interface Interface1 {}

class GenericClass<T,U> where T : SomeClass, Interface1
                        where U : new()
{ ... }
```

Constraints can be applied wherever type parameters are defined, whether in methods or in type definitions.

A *base class constraint* specifies that the type parameter must subclass (or match) a particular class; an *interface constraint* specifies that the type parameter must implement that interface. These constraints allow instances of the type parameter to be implicitly converted to that class or interface.

The *class constraint* and *struct constraint* specify that T must be a reference type or a (non-nullable) value type, respectively. The unmanaged constraint is a stronger version of a struct constraint: T must be a simple value type or a struct that is (recursively) free of any reference types. The *parameterless constructor constraint* requires T to have a public parameterless constructor and allows you to call new() on T:

```
static void Initialize<T> (T[] array) where T : new()
{
  for (int i = 0; i < array.Length; i++)
    array[i] = new T();
}
```

The *naked type constraint* requires one type parameter to derive from (or match) another type parameter.

Subclassing Generic Types

A generic class can be subclassed just like a nongeneric class. The subclass can leave the base class's type parameters open, as in the following example:

```
class Stack<T>                    {...}
class SpecialStack<T> : Stack<T> {...}
```

Or the subclass can close the generic type parameters with a concrete type:

```
class IntStack : Stack<int>  {...}
```

A subtype can also introduce fresh type arguments:

```
class List<T>                       {...}
class KeyedList<T,TKey> : List<T> {...}
```

Self-Referencing Generic Declarations

A type can name *itself* as the concrete type when closing a type argument:

```
public interface IEquatable<T> { bool Equals (T obj); }

public class Balloon : IEquatable<Balloon>
{
  public bool Equals (Balloon b) { ... }
}
```

The following are also legal:

```
class Foo<T> where T : IComparable<T> { ... }
class Bar<T> where T : Bar<T> { ... }
```

Static Data

Static data is unique for each closed type:

```
class Bob<T> { public static int Count; }
...
Console.WriteLine (++Bob<int>.Count);      // 1
Console.WriteLine (++Bob<int>.Count);      // 2
Console.WriteLine (++Bob<string>.Count);   // 1
Console.WriteLine (++Bob<object>.Count);   // 1
```

Covariance

NOTE

Covariance and contravariance are advanced concepts. The motivation behind their introduction into C# was to allow generic interfaces and generics (in particular, those defined in .NET, such as IEnumerable<T>) to work *more as you'd expect*. You can benefit from this without understanding the details behind covariance and contravariance.

Assuming A is convertible to B, X has a covariant type parameter if X<A> is convertible to X<B>.

(With C#'s notion of variance, "convertible" means convertible via an *implicit reference conversion*—such as A *subclassing* B, or A *implementing* B. Numeric conversions, boxing conversions, and custom conversions are not included.)

For instance, type IFoo<T> has a covariant T if the following is legal:

```
IFoo<string> s = ...;
IFoo<object> b = s;
```

Interfaces (and delegates) permit covariant type parameters. To illustrate, suppose that the Stack<T> class that we wrote at the beginning of this section implements the following interface:

```
public interface IPoppable<out T> { T Pop(); }
```

The out modifier on T indicates that T is used only in *output positions* (e.g., return types for methods) and flags the type parameter as *covariant*, permitting the following code:

```
// Assuming that Bear subclasses Animal:
var bears = new Stack<Bear>();
bears.Push (new Bear());

// Because bears implements IPoppable<Bear>,
// we can convert it to IPoppable<Animal>:
IPoppable<Animal> animals = bears;   // Legal
Animal a = animals.Pop();
```

The cast from bears to animals is permitted by the compiler—by virtue of the interface's type parameter being covariant.

NOTE

The IEnumerator<T> and IEnumerable<T> interfaces (see "Enumeration and Iterators" on page 144) are marked with a covariant T. This allows you to cast IEnumerable <string> to IEnumerable<object>, for instance.

The compiler will generate an error if you use a covariant type parameter in an *input* position (e.g., a parameter to a method or a writable property). The purpose of this limitation is to guarantee compile-time type safety. For instance, it prevents us from adding a Push(T) method to that interface, which consumers could abuse with the seemingly benign operation of pushing a camel onto an IPoppable<Animal> (remember that the underlying type in our example is a stack of bears). To define a Push(T) method, T must in fact be *contravariant*.

NOTE

C# supports covariance (and contravariance) only for elements with *reference conversions*—not *boxing conversions*. So, if you wrote a method that accepted a parameter of type IPoppable<object>, you could call it with IPoppable<string>, but not IPoppable<int>.

Contravariance

We previously saw that, assuming that A allows an implicit reference conversion to B, a type X has a covariant type parameter if X<A> allows a reference conversion to X<B>. A type is *contravariant* when you can convert in the reverse direction—from X<B> to X<A>. This is supported on interfaces and delegates when the type parameter appears only in *input* positions, designated with the in modifier. Extending our previous example, if the Stack<T> class implements the following interface:

```
public interface IPushable<in T> { void Push (T obj); }
```

we can legally do this:

```
IPushable<Animal> animals = new Stack<Animal>();
IPushable<Bear> bears = animals;     // Legal
bears.Push (new Bear());
```

Mirroring covariance, the compiler will report an error if you try to use a contravariant type parameter in an output position (e.g., as a return value, or in a readable property).

Delegates

A delegate wires up a method caller to its target method at runtime. There are two aspects to a delegate: *type* and *instance*. A *delegate type* defines a *protocol* to which the caller and target will conform, comprising a list of parameter types and a return type. A *delegate instance* is an object that refers to one (or more) target methods conforming to that protocol.

A delegate instance literally acts as a delegate for the caller: the caller invokes the delegate, and then the delegate calls the target method. This indirection decouples the caller from the target method.

A delegate type declaration is preceded by the keyword dele gate, but otherwise it resembles an (abstract) method declaration. For example:

```
delegate int Transformer (int x);
```

To create a delegate instance, you can assign a method to a delegate variable:

```
class Test
{
  static void Main()
  {
    Transformer t = Square;    // Create delegate instance
    int result = t(3);         // Invoke delegate
    Console.Write (result);    // 9
  }
  static int Square (int x) => x * x;
}
```

Invoking a delegate is just like invoking a method (because the delegate's purpose is merely to provide a level of indirection):

```
t(3);
```

The statement Transformer t = Square is shorthand for the following:

```
Transformer t = new Transformer (Square);
```

And t(3) is shorthand for this:

```
t.Invoke (3);
```

A delegate is similar to a *callback*, a general term that captures constructs such as C function pointers.

Writing Plug-In Methods with Delegates

A delegate variable is assigned a method at runtime. This is useful for writing plug-in methods. In this example, we have a utility method named Transform that applies a transform to each element in an integer array. The Transform method has a delegate parameter for specifying a plug-in transform:

```
public delegate int Transformer (int x);

class Test
{
  static void Main()
  {
    int[] values = { 1, 2, 3 };
    Transform (values, Square);
    foreach (int i in values)
      Console.Write (i + " ");    // 1 4 9
  }

  static void Transform (int[] values, Transformer t)
  {
    for (int i = 0; i < values.Length; i++)
      values[i] = t (values[i]);
  }

  static int Square (int x) => x * x;
}
```

Multicast Delegates

All delegate instances have *multicast* capability. This means that a delegate instance can reference not just a single target method, but also a list of target methods. The + and += operators combine delegate instances. For example:

```
SomeDelegate d = SomeMethod1;
d += SomeMethod2;
```

The last line is functionally the same as this one:

```
d = d + SomeMethod2;
```

Invoking d will now call both SomeMethod1 and SomeMethod2. Delegates are invoked in the order in which they are added.

The - and -= operators remove the right delegate operand from the left delegate operand. For example:

```
d -= SomeMethod1;
```

Invoking d will now cause only SomeMethod2 to be invoked.

Calling + or += on a delegate variable with a null value is legal, as is calling -= on a delegate variable with a single target (which will result in the delegate instance being null).

NOTE

Delegates are *immutable*, so when you call += or -=, you're in fact creating a *new* delegate instance and assigning it to the existing variable.

If a multicast delegate has a nonvoid return type, the caller receives the return value from the last method to be invoked. The preceding methods are still called, but their return values are discarded. In most scenarios in which multicast delegates are used, they have void return types, so this subtlety does not arise.

All delegate types implicitly derive from System.MulticastDelegate, which inherits from System.Delegate. C# compiles +, -, +=, and -= operations made on a delegate to the static Combine and Remove methods of the System.Delegate class.

Instance versus Static Method Targets

When an *instance* method is assigned to a delegate object, the latter must maintain a reference not only to the method, but also to the *instance* to which the method belongs. The Sys tem.Delegate class's Target property represents this instance (and will be null for a delegate referencing a static method).

Generic Delegate Types

A delegate type can contain generic type parameters. For example:

```
public delegate T Transformer<T> (T arg);
```

Here's how we could use this delegate type:

```
static double Square (double x) => x * x;

static void Main()
{
  Transformer<double> s = Square;
  Console.WriteLine (s (3.3));        // 10.89
}
```

The Func and Action Delegates

With generic delegates, it becomes possible to write a small set of delegate types that are so general they can work for methods of any return type and any (reasonable) number of arguments. These delegates are the Func and Action delegates, defined in the System namespace (the in and out annotations indicate *variance*, which we cover in the context of delegates shortly):

```
delegate TResult Func <out TResult> ();
delegate TResult Func <in T, out TResult> (T arg);
delegate TResult Func <in T1, in T2, out TResult>
 (T1 arg1, T2 arg2);
... and so on, up to T16

delegate void Action ();
delegate void Action <in T> (T arg);
delegate void Action <in T1, in T2> (T1 arg1, T2 arg2);
... and so on, up to T16
```

These delegates are extremely general. The `Transformer` delegate in our previous example can be replaced with a `Func` delegate that takes a single argument of type `T` and returns a same-
typed value:

```
public static void Transform<T> (
  T[] values, Func<T,T> transformer)
{
  for (int i = 0; i < values.Length; i++)
    values[i] = transformer (values[i]);
}
```

The only practical scenarios not covered by these delegates are
ref/out and pointer parameters.

Delegate Compatibility

Delegate types are all incompatible with one another, even if
their signatures are the same:

```
delegate void D1(); delegate void D2();
...
D1 d1 = Method1;
D2 d2 = d1;              // Compile-time error
```

The following, however, is permitted:

```
D2 d2 = new D2 (d1);
```

Delegate instances are considered equal if they have the same
type and method target(s). For multicast delegates, the order of
the method targets is significant.

Return type variance

When you call a method, you might get back a type that is
more specific than what you asked for. This is ordinary *polymorphic behavior*. In keeping with this, a delegate target
method might return a more specific type than described by
the delegate. This is *covariance*:

```
delegate object ObjectRetriever();
...
static void Main()
{
```

```
    ObjectRetriever o = new ObjectRetriever (GetString);
    object result = o();
    Console.WriteLine (result);      // hello
}
static string GetString() => "hello";
```

The `ObjectRetriever` expects to get back an `object`, but an `object` *subclass* will also do because delegate return types are *covariant*.

Parameter variance

When you call a method, you can supply arguments that have more specific types than the parameters of that method. This is ordinary polymorphic behavior. In keeping with this, a delegate target method may have *less* specific parameter types than described by the delegate. This is called *contravariance*:

```
delegate void StringAction (string s);
...
static void Main()
{
  StringAction sa = new StringAction (ActOnObject);
  sa ("hello");  // Writes "Hello"
}
static void ActOnObject (object o) => Console.Write (o);
```

NOTE

The standard event pattern is designed to help you take advantage of delegate parameter contravariance through its use of the common `EventArgs` base class. For example, you can have a single method invoked by two different delegates, one passing a `MouseEventArgs` and the other passing a `KeyEventArgs`.

Type parameter variance for generic delegates

We saw in "Generics" on page 108 how type parameters can be covariant and contravariant for generic interfaces. The same capability also exists for generic delegates. If you're defining a generic delegate type, it's a good practice to do the following:

- Mark a type parameter used only on the return value as covariant (out)
- Mark any type parameters used only on parameters as contravariant (in)

Doing so allows conversions to work naturally by respecting inheritance relationships between types. The following delegate (defined in the System namespace) is covariant for TResult

```
delegate TResult Func<out TResult>();
```

allowing:

```
Func<string> x = ...;
Func<object> y = x;
```

The following delegate (defined in the System namespace) is contravariant for T

```
delegate void Action<in T> (T arg);
```

allowing:

```
Action<object> x = ...;
Action<string> y = x;
```

Events

When you're using delegates, two emergent roles commonly appear: *broadcaster* and *subscriber*. The *broadcaster* is a type that contains a delegate field. The broadcaster decides when to broadcast, by invoking the delegate. The *subscribers* are the method target recipients. A subscriber decides when to start and stop listening, by calling += and -= on the broadcaster's delegate. A subscriber does not know about, or interfere with, other subscribers.

Events are a language feature that formalizes this pattern. An event is a construct that exposes just the subset of delegate features required for the broadcaster/subscriber model. The main purpose of events is to *prevent subscribers from interfering with one another*.

The easiest way to declare an event is to put the event keyword in front of a delegate member:

```
public class Broadcaster
{
  public event ProgressReporter Progress;
}
```

Code within the Broadcaster type has full access to Progress and can treat it as a delegate. Code outside of Broadcaster can perform only += and -= operations on the Progress event.

In the following example, the Stock class fires its PriceChanged event every time the Price of the Stock changes:

```
public delegate void PriceChangedHandler
 (decimal oldPrice, decimal newPrice);

public class Stock
{
  string symbol; decimal price;

  public Stock (string symbol) => this.symbol = symbol;

  public event PriceChangedHandler PriceChanged;

  public decimal Price
  {
    get => price;
    set
    {
      if (price == value) return;
      // Fire event if invocation list isn't empty:
      if (PriceChanged != null)
        PriceChanged (price, value);
      price = value;
    }
  }
}
```

If we remove the event keyword from our example so that PriceChanged becomes an ordinary delegate field, our example would give the same results. However, `Stock` would be less robust in that subscribers could do the following things to interfere with one another:

- Replace other subscribers by reassigning `PriceChanged` (instead of using the += operator)
- Clear all subscribers (by setting `PriceChanged` to `null`)
- Broadcast to other subscribers by invoking the delegate

Events can be virtual, overridden, abstract, or sealed. They can also be static.

Standard Event Pattern

In almost all cases in which events are defined in the .NET Core library, their definition adheres to a standard pattern designed to provide consistency across library and user code. Here's the preceding example refactored with this pattern:

```
public class PriceChangedEventArgs : EventArgs
{
  public readonly decimal LastPrice, NewPrice;

  public PriceChangedEventArgs (decimal lastPrice,
                                decimal newPrice)
  {
    LastPrice = lastPrice; NewPrice = newPrice;
  }
}

public class Stock
{
  string symbol; decimal price;

  public Stock (string symbol) => this.symbol = symbol;

  public event EventHandler<PriceChangedEventArgs>
            PriceChanged;

  protected virtual void OnPriceChanged
                    (PriceChangedEventArgs e) =>
```

```
    // Shortcut for invoking PriceChanged if not null:
    PriceChanged?.Invoke (this, e);

  public decimal Price
  {
    get { return price; }
    set
    {
      if (price == value) return;
      OnPriceChanged (new PriceChangedEventArgs (price,
                                                 value));
      price = value;
    }
  }
}
```

At the core of the standard event pattern is System.EventArgs: a predefined .NET class with no members (other than the static Empty property). EventArgs is a base class for conveying information for an event. In this example, we subclass EventArgs to convey the old and new prices when a PriceChanged event is fired.

The generic System.EventHandler delegate is also part of .NET Core and is defined as follows:

```
public delegate void EventHandler<TEventArgs>
  (object source, TEventArgs e)
   where TEventArgs : EventArgs;
```

NOTE

Before C# 2.0 (when generics were added to the language) the solution was to instead write a custom event-handling delegate for each EventArgs type as follows:

```
delegate void PriceChangedHandler
  (object sender,
   PriceChangedEventArgs e);
```

For historical reasons, most events within the .NET libraries use delegates defined in this way.

A protected virtual method named On-*event-name* centralizes firing of the event. This allows subclasses to fire the event (which is usually desirable) and also allows subclasses to insert code before and after the event is fired.

Here's how we could use our Stock class:

```
static void Main()
{
  Stock stock = new Stock ("THPW");
  stock.Price = 27.10M;

  stock.PriceChanged += stock_PriceChanged;
  stock.Price = 31.59M;
}

static void stock_PriceChanged
  (object sender, PriceChangedEventArgs e)
{
  if ((e.NewPrice - e.LastPrice) / e.LastPrice > 0.1M)
    Console.WriteLine ("Alert, 10% price increase!");
}
```

For events that don't carry additional information, .NET also provides a nongeneric EventHandler delegate. We can demonstrate this by rewriting our Stock class such that the Price Changed event fires *after* the price changes. This means that no additional information need be transmitted with the event:

```
public class Stock
{
  string symbol; decimal price;

  public Stock (string symbol) => this.symbol = symbol;

  public event EventHandler PriceChanged;

  protected virtual void OnPriceChanged (EventArgs e) =>
    PriceChanged?.Invoke (this, e);

  public decimal Price
  {
    get => price;
    set
    {
```

```
      if (price == value) return;
      price = value;
      OnPriceChanged (EventArgs.Empty);
    }
  }
}
```

Note that we also used the `EventArgs.Empty` property—this saves instantiating an instance of `EventArgs`.

Event Accessors

An event's *accessors* are the implementations of its += and -= functions. By default, accessors are implemented implicitly by the compiler. Consider this event declaration:

```
public event EventHandler PriceChanged;
```

The compiler converts this to the following:

- A private delegate field
- A public pair of event accessor functions, whose implementations forward the += and -= operations to the private delegate field

You can take over this process by defining *explicit* event accessors. Here's a manual implementation of the `PriceChanged` event from our previous example:

```
EventHandler priceChanged;   // Private delegate
public event EventHandler PriceChanged
{
  add    { priceChanged += value; }
  remove { priceChanged -= value; }
}
```

This example is functionally identical to C#'s default accessor implementation (except that C# also ensures thread safety around updating the delegate). By defining event accessors ourselves, we instruct C# not to generate default field and accessor logic.

With explicit event accessors, you can apply more complex strategies to the storage and access of the underlying delegate. This is useful when the event accessors are merely relays for another class that is broadcasting the event, or when explicitly implementing an interface that declares an event:

```
public interface IFoo { event EventHandler Ev; }
class Foo : IFoo
{
  EventHandler ev;
  event EventHandler IFoo.Ev
  {
    add { ev += value; } remove { ev -= value; }
  }
}
```

Lambda Expressions

A lambda expression is an unnamed method written in place of a delegate instance. The compiler immediately converts the lambda expression to either of the following:

- A delegate instance.
- An *expression tree*, of type Expression<TDelegate>, representing the code inside the lambda expression in a traversable object model. This allows the lambda expression to be interpreted later at runtime (we describe the process in Chapter 8 of *C# 8.0 in a Nutshell*).

Given the following delegate type

```
delegate int Transformer (int i);
```

we could assign and invoke the lambda expression x => x * x as follows:

```
Transformer sqr = x => x * x;
Console.WriteLine (sqr(3));    // 9
```

A lambda expression has the following form:

```
(parameters) => expression-or-statement-block
```

For convenience, you can omit the parentheses if and only if there is exactly one parameter of an inferable type.

In our example, there is a single parameter, x, and the expression is x * x:

```
x => x * x;
```

Each parameter of the lambda expression corresponds to a delegate parameter, and the type of the expression (which can be void) corresponds to the return type of the delegate.

In our example, x corresponds to parameter i, and the expression x * x corresponds to the return type int, therefore being compatible with the Transformer delegate.

A lambda expression's code can be a *statement block* instead of an expression. We can rewrite our example as follows:

```
x => { return x * x; };
```

Lambda expressions are used most commonly with the Func and Action delegates, so you will most often see our earlier expression written as follows:

```
Func<int,int> sqr = x => x * x;
```

The compiler can usually *infer* the type of lambda parameters contextually. When this is not the case, you can specify parameter types explicitly:

```
Func<int,int> sqr = (int x) => x * x;
```

Here's an example of an expression that accepts two parameters:

```
Func<string,string,int> totalLength =
  (s1, s2) => s1.Length + s2.Length;

int total = totalLength ("hello", "world");  // total=10;
```

Assuming `Clicked` is an event of type `EventHandler`, the following attaches an event handler via a lambda expression:

```
obj.Clicked += (sender,args) => Console.Write ("Click");
```

Capturing Outer Variables

A lambda expression can reference the local variables and parameters of the method in which it's defined (*outer variables*). For example:

```
static void Main()
{
  int factor = 2;
  Func<int, int> multiplier = n => n * factor;
  Console.WriteLine (multiplier (3));          // 6
}
```

Outer variables referenced by a lambda expression are called *captured variables*. A lambda expression that captures variables is called a *closure*. Captured variables are evaluated when the delegate is actually *invoked*, not when the variables were *captured*:

```
int factor = 2;
Func<int, int> multiplier = n => n * factor;
factor = 10;
Console.WriteLine (multiplier (3));          // 30
```

Lambda expressions can themselves update captured variables:

```
int seed = 0;
Func<int> natural = () => seed++;
Console.WriteLine (natural());               // 0
Console.WriteLine (natural());               // 1
Console.WriteLine (seed);                    // 2
```

Captured variables have their lifetimes extended to that of the delegate. In the following example, the local variable seed would ordinarily disappear from scope when Natural finished executing. But because seed has been *captured*, its lifetime is extended to that of the capturing delegate, natural:

```
static Func<int> Natural()
{
  int seed = 0;
  return () => seed++;         // Returns a closure
}
static void Main()
{
  Func<int> natural = Natural();
  Console.WriteLine (natural());        // 0
  Console.WriteLine (natural());        // 1
}
```

NOTE

Variables can also be captured by anonymous methods and local methods. The rules for captured variables, in these cases, are the same.

Capturing iteration variables

When you capture an iteration variable in a for loop, C# treats the iteration variable as though it were declared *outside* the loop. This means that the *same* variable is captured in each iteration. The following program writes 333 instead of writing 012:

```
Action[] actions = new Action[3];

for (int i = 0; i < 3; i++)
  actions [i] = () => Console.Write (i);

foreach (Action a in actions) a();        // 333
```

Each closure (shown in boldface) captures the same variable, i. (This actually makes sense when you consider that i is a variable whose value persists between loop iterations; you can even explicitly change i within the loop body if you want.) The consequence is that when the delegates are later invoked, each delegate sees i's value at the time of *invocation*—which is 3. The solution, if we want to write 012, is to assign the iteration variable to a local variable that's scoped *within* the loop:

```
Action[] actions = new Action[3];
for (int i = 0; i < 3; i++)
{
  int loopScopedi = i;
  actions [i] = () => Console.Write (loopScopedi);
}
foreach (Action a in actions) a();      // 012
```

This causes the closure to capture a *different* variable on each iteration.

NOTE

foreach loops used to work in the same way, but the rules have since changed. Starting with C# 5.0, you can safely close over a foreach loop's iteration variable without needing a temporary variable.

Lambda Expressions versus Local Methods

The functionality of local methods (see "Local methods" on page 70) overlaps with that of lambda expressions. Local methods have the advantages of allowing for recursion and avoiding the clutter of specifying a delegate. Avoiding the indirection of a delegate also makes them slightly more efficient, and they can access local variables of the containing method without the compiler having to "hoist" the captured variables into a hidden class.

However, in many cases you *need* a delegate, most commonly when calling a higher-order function (i.e., a method with a delegate-typed parameter):

```
public void Foo (Func<int,bool> predicate) { ... }
```

In such cases, you need a delegate anyway, and it's precisely in these cases that lambda expressions are usually terser and cleaner.

Anonymous Methods

Anonymous methods are a C# 2.0 feature that has been mostly subsumed by lambda expressions. An anonymous method is like a lambda expression except that it lacks implicitly typed parameters, expression syntax (an anonymous method must always be a statement block), and the ability to compile to an expression tree. To write an anonymous method, you include the `delegate` keyword followed (optionally) by a parameter declaration and then a method body. For example, given this delegate

```
delegate int Transformer (int i);
```

we could write and call an anonymous method as follows:

```
Transformer sqr = delegate (int x) {return x * x;};
Console.WriteLine (sqr(3));          // 9
```

The first line is semantically equivalent to the following lambda expression:

```
Transformer sqr =       (int x) => {return x * x;};
```

Or simply:

```
Transformer sqr =       x  => x * x;
```

A unique feature of anonymous methods is that you can omit the parameter declaration entirely—even if the delegate expects it. This can be useful in declaring events with a default empty handler:

```
public event EventHandler Clicked = delegate { };
```

This avoids the need for a null check before firing the event. The following is also legal (notice the lack of parameters):

```
Clicked += delegate { Console.Write ("clicked"); };
```

Anonymous methods capture outer variables in the same way lambda expressions do.

try Statements and Exceptions

A try statement specifies a code block subject to error-handling or cleanup code. The try *block* must be followed by one or more catch *blocks*, and/or a finally *block*. The catch block executes when an error is thrown in the try block. The finally block executes after execution leaves the try block (or if present, the catch block), to perform cleanup code, whether or not an exception was thrown.

A catch block has access to an Exception object that contains information about the error. You use a catch block to either compensate for the error or *rethrow* the exception. You rethrow an exception if you merely want to log the problem, or if you want to rethrow a new, higher-level exception type.

A finally block adds determinism to your program by always executing no matter what. It's useful for cleanup tasks such as closing network connections.

A try statement looks like this:

```
try
{
  ... // exception may get thrown within execution of
      // this block
}
catch (ExceptionA ex)
{
  ... // handle exception of type ExceptionA
}
catch (ExceptionB ex)
{
  ... // handle exception of type ExceptionB
}
finally
{
  ... // cleanup code
}
```

Consider the following code:

```
int x = 3, y = 0;
Console.WriteLine (x / y);
```

Because y is zero, the runtime throws a DivideByZeroException and our program terminates. We can prevent this by catching the exception as follows:

```
Try
{
  int x = 3, y = 0;
  Console.WriteLine (x / y);
}
catch (DivideByZeroException ex)
{
  Console.Write ("y cannot be zero. ");
}
// Execution resumes here after exception...
```

NOTE

This is a simple example to illustrate exception handling. We could deal with this particular scenario better in practice by checking explicitly for the divisor being zero before calling Calc.

Exceptions are relatively expensive to handle, taking hundreds of clock cycles.

When an exception is thrown within a try statement, the CLR performs a test:

Does the try *statement have any compatible* catch *blocks?*

- If so, execution jumps to the compatible catch block, followed by the finally block (if present), and then execution continues normally.

- If not, execution jumps directly to the finally block (if present), and the CLR looks up the call stack for other try blocks and, if found, repeats the test.

If no function in the call stack takes responsibility for the exception, an error dialog is displayed to the user, and the program terminates.

The catch Clause

A catch clause specifies what type of exception to catch. This must be either System.Exception or a subclass of System.Exception. Catching System.Exception snares all possible errors. This is useful when:

- Your program can potentially recover regardless of the specific exception type.
- You plan to rethrow the exception (perhaps after logging it).
- Your error handler is the last resort, prior to termination of the program.

More typically, though, you catch *specific exception types* in order to avoid having to deal with circumstances for which your handler wasn't designed (e.g., an OutOfMemoryException).

You can handle multiple exception types with multiple catch clauses:

```
try
{
  DoSomething();
}
catch (IndexOutOfRangeException ex) { ... }
catch (FormatException ex)          { ... }
catch (OverflowException ex)        { ... }
```

Only one catch clause executes for a given exception. If you want to include a safety net to catch more general exceptions (such as System.Exception), you must put the more specific handlers *first*.

You can catch an exception without specifying a variable, if you don't need to access its properties:

```
catch (OverflowException)    // no variable
{ ... }
```

Furthermore, you can omit both the variable and the type (meaning that all exceptions will be caught):

```
catch { ... }
```

Exception filters

From C# 6.0, you can specify an *exception filter* in a catch clause by adding a when clause:

```
catch (WebException ex)
  when (ex.Status == WebExceptionStatus.Timeout)
{
  ...
}
```

If a WebException is thrown in this example, the Boolean expression following the when keyword is then evaluated. If the result is false, the catch block in question is ignored, and any subsequent catch clauses are considered. With exception filters, it can be meaningful to catch the same exception type again:

```
catch (WebException ex) when (ex.Status == something)
{ ... }
catch (WebException ex) when (ex.Status == somethingelse)
{ ... }
```

The Boolean expression in the when clause can be side-effecting, such as a method that logs the exception for diagnostic purposes.

The finally Block

A finally block always executes—whether or not an exception is thrown and whether or not the try block runs to completion. finally blocks are typically used for cleanup code.

A `finally` block executes either:

- After a `catch` block finishes
- After control leaves the `try` block because of a jump statement (e.g., `return` or `goto`)
- After the `try` block ends

A `finally` block helps add determinism to a program. In the following example, the file that we open *always* gets closed, regardless of whether:

- The `try` block finishes normally
- Execution returns early because the file is empty (`EndOf Stream`)
- An `IOException` is thrown while the file is being read

For example:

```
static void ReadFile()
{
  StreamReader reader = null;  // In System.IO namespace
  try
  {
    reader = File.OpenText ("file.txt");
    if (reader.EndOfStream) return;
    Console.WriteLine (reader.ReadToEnd());
  }
  finally
  {
    if (reader != null) reader.Dispose();
  }
}
```

In this example, we closed the file by calling `Dispose` on the `StreamReader`. Calling `Dispose` on an object, within a `finally` block, is a standard convention throughout .NET and is supported explicitly in C# through the `using` statement.

The using statement

Many classes encapsulate unmanaged resources such as file handles, graphics handles, or database connections. These classes implement System.IDisposable, which defines a single parameterless method named Dispose to clean up these resources. The using statement provides an elegant syntax for calling Dispose on an IDisposable object within a finally block.

The following

```
using (StreamReader reader = File.OpenText ("file.txt"))
{
  ...
}
```

is precisely equivalent to:

```
{
  StreamReader reader = File.OpenText ("file.txt");
  try
  {
    ...
  }
  finally
  {
    if (reader != null) ((IDisposable)reader).Dispose();
  }
}
```

using declarations (C# 8)

If you omit the brackets and statement block following a using statement, it becomes a *using declaration*. The resource is then disposed when execution falls outside the *enclosing* statement block:

```
if (File.Exists ("file.txt"))
{
  using var reader = File.OpenText ("file.txt");
  Console.WriteLine (reader.ReadLine());
  ...
}
```

In this case, reader will be disposed when execution falls outside the if statement block.

Throwing Exceptions

Exceptions can be thrown either by the runtime or in user code. In this example, Display throws a System.ArgumentNull Exception:

```
static void Display (string name)
{
  if (name == null)
    throw new ArgumentNullException (nameof (name));

  Console.WriteLine (name);
}
```

throw expressions

From C# 7, throw can appear as an expression in expression-bodied functions:

```
public string Foo() => throw new
NotImplementedException();
```

A throw expression can also appear in a ternary conditional expression:

```
string ProperCase (string value) =>
  value == null ? throw new ArgumentException ("value") :
  value == "" ? "" :
  char.ToUpper (value[0]) + value.Substring (1);
```

Rethrowing an exception

You can capture and rethrow an exception as follows:

```
try { ... }
catch (Exception ex)
{
  // Log error
  ...
  throw;          // Rethrow same exception
}
```

Rethrowing in this manner lets you log an error without *swallowing* it. It also lets you back out of handling an exception should circumstances turn out to be outside what you expected.

NOTE

If we replaced throw with throw ex, the example would still work, but the StackTrace property of the exception would no longer reflect the original error.

The other common scenario is to rethrow a more specific or meaningful exception type:

```
try
{
    ... // parse a date of birth from XML element data
}
catch (FormatException ex)
{
    throw new XmlException ("Invalid date of birth", ex);
}
```

When rethrowing a different exception, you can populate the InnerException property with the original exception to aid debugging. Nearly all types of exceptions provide a constructor for this purpose (such as in our example).

Key Properties of System.Exception

The most important properties of System.Exception are the following:

StackTrace
> A string representing all the methods that are called from the origin of the exception to the catch block.

Message
> A string with a description of the error.

InnerException

> The inner exception (if any) that caused the outer exception. This, itself, might have another `InnerException`.

Common Exception Types

The following exception types are used widely throughout the CLR and .NET; you can throw them yourself or use them as base classes for deriving custom exception types:

System.ArgumentException

> Thrown when a function is called with a bogus argument. This generally indicates a program bug.

System.ArgumentNullException

> Subclass of `ArgumentException` that's thrown when a function argument is (unexpectedly) `null`.

System.ArgumentOutOfRangeException

> Subclass of `ArgumentException` that's thrown when a (usually numeric) argument is too big or too small. For example, this is thrown when you pass a negative number into a function that accepts only positive values.

System.InvalidOperationException

> Thrown when the state of an object is unsuitable for a method to successfully execute, regardless of any particular argument values. Examples include reading an unopened file or getting the next element from an enumerator where the underlying list has been modified partway through the iteration.

System.NotSupportedException

> Thrown to indicate that a particular functionality is not supported. A good example is calling the `Add` method on a collection for which `IsReadOnly` returns `true`.

System.NotImplementedException

> Thrown to indicate that a function has not yet been implemented.

```
System.ObjectDisposedException
```
Thrown when the object upon which the function is called has been disposed.

Enumeration and Iterators

Enumeration

An *enumerator* is a read-only, forward-only cursor over a *sequence of values*. An enumerator is an object that implements `System.Collections.IEnumerator` or `System.Collections.Generic.IEnumerator<T>`.

The `foreach` statement iterates over an *enumerable* object. An enumerable object is the logical representation of a sequence. It is not itself a cursor, but an object that produces cursors over itself. An enumerable either implements `IEnumerable`/`IEnumerable<T>` or has a method named `GetEnumerator` that returns an *enumerator*.

The enumeration pattern is as follows:

```
class Enumerator   // Typically implements IEnumerator<T>
{
  public IteratorVariableType Current { get {...} }
  public bool MoveNext() {...}
}
class Enumerable   // Typically implements IEnumerable<T>
{
  public Enumerator GetEnumerator() {...}
}
```

Here is the high-level way to iterate through the characters in the word *beer* using a `foreach` statement:

```
foreach (char c in "beer") Console.WriteLine (c);
```

Here is the low-level way to iterate through the characters in *beer* without using a `foreach` statement:

```
using (var enumerator = "beer".GetEnumerator())
  while (enumerator.MoveNext())
  {
    var element = enumerator.Current;
```

```
    Console.WriteLine (element);
  }
```

If the enumerator implements IDisposable, the foreach state-ment also acts as a using statement, implicitly disposing the enumerator object.

Collection Initializers

You can instantiate and populate an enumerable object in a sin-gle step. For example:

```
using System.Collections.Generic;
...

List<int> list = new List<int> {1, 2, 3};
```

The compiler translates the last line into the following:

```
List<int> list = new List<int>();
list.Add (1); list.Add (2); list.Add (3);
```

This requires that the enumerable object implements the System.Collections.IEnumerable interface, and that it has an Add method that has the appropriate number of parameters for the call. You can similarly initialize dictionaries (types that implement System.Collections.IDictionary) as follows:

```
var dict = new Dictionary<int, string>()
{
  { 5, "five" },
  { 10, "ten" }
};
```

Or, more succinctly:

```
var dict = new Dictionary<int, string>()
{
  [5] = "five",
  [10] = "ten"
};
```

The latter is valid not only with dictionaries, but with any type for which an indexer exists.

Iterators

Whereas a foreach statement is a *consumer* of an enumerator, an iterator is a *producer* of an enumerator. In this example, we use an iterator to return a sequence of Fibonacci numbers (for which each number is the sum of the previous two):

```
using System;
using System.Collections.Generic;

class Test
{
  static void Main()
  {
    foreach (int fib in Fibs(6))
      Console.Write (fib + "  ");
  }

  static IEnumerable<int> Fibs(int fibCount)
  {
    for (int i = 0, prevFib = 1, curFib = 1;
         i < fibCount;
         i++)
    {
      yield return prevFib;
      int newFib = prevFib+curFib;
      prevFib = curFib;
      curFib = newFib;
    }
  }
}
OUTPUT: 1  1  2  3  5  8
```

Whereas a return statement expresses, "Here's the value you asked me to return from this method," a yield return statement expresses, "Here's the next element you asked me to yield from this enumerator." On each yield statement, control is returned to the caller, but the callee's state is maintained so that the method can continue executing as soon as the caller enumerates the next element. The lifetime of this state is bound to the enumerator, such that the state can be released when the caller has finished enumerating.

Iterator Semantics

An iterator is a method, property, or indexer that contains one or more yield statements. An iterator must return one of the following four interfaces (otherwise, the compiler will generate an error):

```
System.Collections.IEnumerable
System.Collections.IEnumerator
System.Collections.Generic.IEnumerable<T>
System.Collections.Generic.IEnumerator<T>
```

Iterators that return an *enumerator* interface tend to be used less often. They're useful when you're writing a custom collection class: typically, you name the iterator GetEnumerator and have your class implement IEnumerable<T>.

Iterators that return an *enumerable* interface are more common —and simpler to use because you don't need to write a collection class. The compiler, behind the scenes, writes a private class implementing IEnumerable<T> (as well as IEnumerator<T>).

Multiple yield statements

An iterator can include multiple yield statements:

```
static void Main()
{
  foreach (string s in Foo())
    Console.Write (s + " ");      // One Two Three
}

static IEnumerable<string> Foo()
{
  yield return "One";
  yield return "Two";
  yield return "Three";
}
```

yield break

A return statement is illegal in an iterator block; instead you must use the yield break statement to indicate that the iterator block should exit early, without returning more elements. We can modify Foo as follows to demonstrate:

```
static IEnumerable<string> Foo (bool breakEarly)
{
  yield return "One";
  yield return "Two";
  if (breakEarly) yield break;
  yield return "Three";
}
```

Composing Sequences

Iterators are highly composable. We can extend our Fibonacci example by adding the following method to the class:

```
static IEnumerable<int> EvenNumbersOnly (
  IEnumerable<int> sequence)
  {
    foreach (int x in sequence)
      if ((x % 2) == 0)
        yield return x;
  }
}
```

We can then output even Fibonacci numbers as follows:

```
foreach (int fib in EvenNumbersOnly (Fibs (6)))
  Console.Write (fib + " ");   // 2 8
```

Each element is not calculated until the last moment—when requested by a MoveNext() operation. Figure 5 shows the data requests and data output over time.

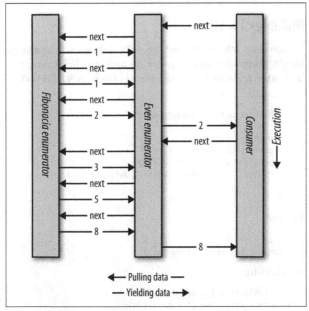

Figure 5. Composing sequences

The composability of the iterator pattern is essential in building LINQ queries.

Nullable (Value) Types

Reference types can represent a nonexistent value with a null reference. Value types, however, cannot ordinarily represent null values. For example:

```
string s = null;    // OK - reference type.
int i = null;       // Compile error - int cannot be null.
```

To represent null in a value type, you must use a special construct called a *nullable type*. A nullable type is denoted with a value type followed by the ? symbol:

```
int? i = null;                        // OK - Nullable Type
Console.WriteLine (i == null);        // True
```

Nullable<T> Struct

T? translates into System.Nullable<T>. Nullable<T> is a lightweight immutable structure, having only two fields, to represent Value and HasValue. The essence of System.Nullable<T> is very simple:

```
public struct Nullable<T> where T : struct
{
  public T Value {get;}
  public bool HasValue {get;}
  public T GetValueOrDefault();
  public T GetValueOrDefault (T defaultValue);
  ...
}
```

The code

```
int? i = null;
Console.WriteLine (i == null);        // True
```

translates to:

```
Nullable<int> i = new Nullable<int>();
Console.WriteLine (! i.HasValue);     // True
```

Attempting to retrieve Value when HasValue is false throws an InvalidOperationException. GetValueOrDefault() returns Value if HasValue is true; otherwise, it returns new T() or a specified custom default value.

The default value of T? is null.

Nullable Conversions

The conversion from T to T? is implicit, and from T? to T is explicit. For example:

```
int? x = 5;        // implicit
int y = (int)x;    // explicit
```

The explicit cast is directly equivalent to calling the nullable object's Value property. Hence, an InvalidOperationException is thrown if HasValue is false.

Boxing/Unboxing Nullable Values

When T? is boxed, the boxed value on the heap contains T, not T?. This optimization is possible because a boxed value is a reference type that can already express null.

C# also permits the unboxing of nullable types with the as operator. The result will be null if the cast fails:

```
object o = "string";
int? x = o as int?;
Console.WriteLine (x.HasValue);   // False
```

Operator Lifting

The Nullable<T> struct does not define operators such as <, >, or even ==. Despite this, the following code compiles and executes correctly:

```
int? x = 5;
int? y = 10;
bool b = x < y;    // true
```

This works because the compiler borrows or "lifts" the less-than operator from the underlying value type. Semantically, it translates the preceding comparison expression into this:

```
bool b = (x.HasValue && y.HasValue)
         ? (x.Value < y.Value)
         : false;
```

In other words, if both x and y have values, it compares via int's less-than operator; otherwise, it returns false.

Operator lifting means that you can implicitly use T's operators on T?. You can define operators for T? in order to provide special-purpose null behavior, but in the vast majority of cases, it's best to rely on the compiler automatically applying systematic nullable logic for you.

The compiler performs null logic differently depending on the category of operator.

Equality operators (==, !=)

Lifted equality operators handle nulls just like reference types do. This means two null values are equal:

```
Console.WriteLine (        null ==        null);  // True
Console.WriteLine ((bool?)null == (bool?)null);  // True
```

Further:

- If exactly one operand is null, the operands are unequal.
- If both operands are non-null, their Values are compared.

Relational operators (<, <=, >=, >)

The relational operators work on the principle that it is meaningless to compare null operands. This means that comparing a null value to either a null or a non-null value returns false:

```
bool b = x < y;    // Translation:

bool b = (x == null || y == null)
  ? false
  : (x.Value < y.Value);

// b is false (assuming x is 5 and y is null)
```

All other operators (+, −, *, /, %, &, |, ^, <<, >>, +, ++, --, !, ~)

These operators return null when any of the operands are null. This pattern should be familiar to SQL users.

```
int? c = x + y;    // Translation:

int? c = (x == null || y == null)
         ? null
         : (int?) (x.Value + y.Value);

// c is null (assuming x is 5 and y is null)
```

An exception is when the & and | operators are applied to bool?, which we discuss shortly.

Mixing nullable and non-nullable operators

You can mix and match nullable and non-nullable types (this works because there is an implicit conversion from T to T?):

```
int? a = null;
int b = 2;
int? c = a + b;    // c is null - equivalent to a +
(int?)b
```

bool? with & and | Operators

When supplied operands of type bool?, the & and | operators treat null as an *unknown value*. So, null | true is true, because:

- If the unknown value is false, the result would be true.
- If the unknown value is true, the result would be true.

Similarly, null & false is false. This behavior would be familiar to SQL users. The following example enumerates other combinations:

```
bool? n = null, f = false, t = true;
Console.WriteLine (n | n);    // (null)
Console.WriteLine (n | f);    // (null)
Console.WriteLine (n | t);    // True
Console.WriteLine (n & n);    // (null)
Console.WriteLine (n & f);    // False
Console.WriteLine (n & t);    // (null)
```

Nullable Types and Null Operators

Nullable types work particularly well with the ?? operator (see "Null-Coalescing Operator" on page 51). For example:

```
int? x = null;
int y = x ?? 5;        // y is 5

int? a = null, b = null, c = 123;
Console.WriteLine (a ?? b ?? c);  // 123
```

Using ?? on a nullable value type is equivalent to calling GetValueOrDefault with an explicit default value, except that the expression for the default value is never evaluated if the variable is not null.

Nullable types also work well with the null-conditional operator (see "Null-Conditional Operator" on page 51). In the following example, length evaluates to null:

```
System.Text.StringBuilder sb = null;
int? length = sb?.ToString().Length;
```

We can combine this with the null-coalescing operator to evaluate to zero instead of null:

```
int length = sb?.ToString().Length ?? 0;
```

Nullable Reference Types (C# 8)

Whereas *nullable types* bring nullability to value types, *nullable reference types* do the opposite and bring (a degree of) *non-nullability* to reference types, with the purpose of helping to avoid NullReferenceExceptions.

Nullable reference types introduce a level of safety that's enforced purely by the compiler in the form of warnings when it detects code that's at risk of generating a NullReferenceException.

To enable nullable reference types, you must either add the Nullable element to your *.csproj* project file (if you want to enable it for the entire project)

```
<Nullable>enable</Nullable>
```

or/and use the following directives in your code, in the places
where it should take effect:

```
#nullable enable    // enables NRT from this point on
#nullable disable   // disables NRT from this point on
#nullable restore   // resets NRT to project setting
```

After it is enabled, the compiler makes non-nullability the
default: If you want a reference type to accept nulls, you must
apply the ? suffix to indicate a *nullable reference type*. In the following example, s1 is non-nullable, whereas s2 is nullable:

```
#nullable enable    // Enable nullable reference types

string s1 = null;   // Generates a compiler warning!
string? s2 = null;  // OK: s2 is nullable reference type
```

NOTE

Because nullable reference types are compile-time constructs, there's no runtime difference between string and
string?. In contrast, nullable (value) types introduce
something concrete into the type system, namely the
Nullable<T> struct.

The following also generates a warning because x is not
initialized:

```
class Foo { string x; }
```

The warning disappears if you initialize x, either via a field initializer or via code in the constructor.

The compiler also warns you upon dereferencing a nullable reference type if it thinks a NullReferenceException might occur.
In the following example, accessing the string's Length property
generates a warning:

```
void Foo (string? s) => Console.Write (s.Length);
```

To remove the warning, you can use the *null-forgiving operator* (!):

```
void Foo (string? s) => Console.Write (s!.Length);
```

Our use of the null-forgiving operator in this example is dangerous in that we could end up throwing the very NullReferenceException we were trying to avoid in the first place. We could fix it as follows:

```
void Foo (string? s)
{
  if (s != null) Console.Write (s.Length);
}
```

Notice now, that we don't need the null-forgiving operator. This is because the compiler performs static analysis and is smart enough to infer—at least in simple cases—when a dereference is safe and there's no chance of a NullReferenceException.

The compiler's ability to detect and warn is not bullet-proof, and there are also limits to what's possible in terms of coverage. For instance, it's unable to know whether an array's elements have been populated, and so the following does not generate a warning:

```
var strings = new string[10];
Console.WriteLine (strings[0].Length);
```

Extension Methods

Extension methods allow an existing type to be extended with new methods, without altering the definition of the original type. An extension method is a static method of a static class, where the this modifier is applied to the first parameter. The type of the first parameter will be the type that is extended. For example:

```
public static class StringHelper
{
  public static bool IsCapitalized (this string s)
  {
    if (string.IsNullOrEmpty (s)) return false;
```

```
      return char.IsUpper (s[0]);
  }
}
```

The IsCapitalized extension method can be called as though it were an instance method on a string, as follows:

```
Console.Write ("Perth".IsCapitalized());
```

An extension method call, when compiled, is translated back into an ordinary static method call:

```
Console.Write (StringHelper.IsCapitalized ("Perth"));
```

Interfaces can be extended, too:

```
public static T First<T> (this IEnumerable<T> sequence)
{
   foreach (T element in sequence)
     return element;
   throw new InvalidOperationException ("No elements!");
}
...
Console.WriteLine ("Seattle".First());   // S
```

Extension Method Chaining

Extension methods, like instance methods, provide a tidy way to chain functions. Consider the following two functions:

```
public static class StringHelper
{
   public static string Pluralize (this string s) {...}
   public static string Capitalize (this string s) {...}
}
```

x and y are equivalent, and both evaluate to "Sausages", but x uses extension methods, whereas y uses static methods:

```
string x = "sausage".Pluralize().Capitalize();

string y = StringHelper.Capitalize
            (StringHelper.Pluralize ("sausage"));
```

Ambiguity and Resolution

Namespaces

An extension method cannot be accessed unless the namespace is in scope (typically imported with a using statement).

Extension methods versus instance methods

Any compatible instance method will always take precedence over an extension method—even when the extension method's parameters are more specifically type-matched.

Extension methods versus extension methods

If two extension methods have the same signature, the extension method must be called as an ordinary static method to disambiguate the method to call. If one extension method has more specific arguments, however, the more specific method takes precedence.

Anonymous Types

An anonymous type is a simple class created on the fly to store a set of values. To create an anonymous type, you use the new keyword followed by an object initializer, specifying the properties and values the type will contain. For example:

```
var dude = new { Name = "Bob", Age = 1 };
```

The compiler resolves this by writing a private nested type with read-only properties for Name (type string) and Age (type int). You must use the var keyword to reference an anonymous type, because the type's name is compiler-generated.

The property name of an anonymous type can be inferred from an expression that is itself an identifier; thus

```
int Age = 1;
var dude = new { Name = "Bob", Age };
```

is equivalent to:

```
var dude = new { Name = "Bob", Age = Age };
```

You can create arrays of anonymous types as follows:

```
var dudes = new[]
{
  new { Name = "Bob", Age = 30 },
  new { Name = "Mary", Age = 40 }
};
```

Anonymous types are used primarily when you're writing LINQ queries.

Tuples

Like anonymous types, tuples (C# 7+) provide a simple way to store a set of values. The main purpose of tuples is to safely return multiple values from a method without resorting to out parameters (something you cannot do with anonymous types). The simplest way to create a *tuple literal* is to list the desired values in parentheses. This creates a tuple with *unnamed* elements:

```
var bob = ("Bob", 23);
Console.WriteLine (bob.Item1);    // Bob
Console.WriteLine (bob.Item2);    // 23
```

Unlike with anonymous types, var is optional and you can specify a *tuple type* explicitly:

```
(string,int) bob  = ("Bob", 23);
```

This means that you can usefully return a tuple from a method:

```
static (string,int) GetPerson() => ("Bob", 23);

static void Main()
{
  (string,int) person = GetPerson();
  Console.WriteLine (person.Item1);   // Bob
  Console.WriteLine (person.Item2);   // 23
}
```

Tuples play well with generics, so the following types are all legal:

```
Task<(string,int)>
Dictionary<(string,int),Uri>
IEnumerable<(int ID, string Name)>   // See below...
```

Tuples are *value types* with *mutable* (read/write) elements. This means that you can modify Item1, Item2, and so on, after creating a tuple.

Naming Tuple Elements

You can optionally give meaningful names to elements when creating tuple literals:

```
var tuple = (Name:"Bob", Age:23);
Console.WriteLine (tuple.Name);      // Bob
Console.WriteLine (tuple.Age);       // 23
```

You can do the same when specifying *tuple types*:

```
static (string Name, int Age) GetPerson() => ("Bob",23);
```

Element names are automatically *inferred* from property or field names:

```
var now = DateTime.Now;
var tuple = (now.Day, now.Month, now.Year);
Console.WriteLine (tuple.Day);                    // OK
```

NOTE

Tuples are syntactic sugar for using a family of generic structs called ValueTuple<T1>, ValueTuple<T1,T2>, which have fields named Item1, Item2, and so on. Hence (string,int) is an alias for ValueTuple<string,int>. This means that "named elements" exist only in the source code—and the imagination of the compiler—and mostly disappear at runtime.

```
```

Deconstructing Tuples

Tuples implicitly support the deconstruction pattern (see "Deconstructors" on page 72), so you can easily *deconstruct* a tuple into individual variables. So, instead of this

```
var bob = ("Bob", 23);
string name = bob.Item1;
int age = bob.Item2;
```

you can do this:

```
var bob = ("Bob", 23);
(string name, int age) = bob;    // Deconstruct bob into
                                 // name and age.
Console.WriteLine (name);
Console.WriteLine (age);
```

The syntax for deconstruction is confusingly similar to the syntax for declaring a tuple with named elements! The following highlights the difference:

```
(string name, int age)      = bob;  // Deconstructing
(string name, int age) bob2 = bob;  // Declaring tuple
```

LINQ

LINQ, or Language Integrated Query, allows you to write structured type-safe queries over local object collections and remote data sources.

LINQ lets you query any collection implementing IEnumerable<>, whether an array, list, XML DOM, or remote data source (such as a table in SQL Server). LINQ offers the benefits of both compile-time type checking and dynamic query composition.

LINQ Fundamentals

The basic units of data in LINQ are *sequences* and *elements*. A sequence is any object that implements the generic `IEnumerable` interface, and an element is each item in the sequence. In the following example, `names` is a sequence, and `Tom`, `Dick`, and `Harry` are elements:

```
string[] names = { "Tom", "Dick", "Harry" };
```

A sequence such as this we call a *local sequence* because it represents a local collection of objects in memory.

A *query operator* is a method that transforms a sequence. A typical query operator accepts an *input sequence* and emits a transformed *output sequence*. In the `Enumerable` class in `System.Linq`, there are around 40 query operators, all implemented as static extension methods. These are called *standard query operators*.

NOTE

LINQ also supports sequences that can be dynamically fed from a remote data source such as SQL Server. These sequences additionally implement the `IQueryable<>` interface and are supported through a matching set of standard query operators in the `Queryable` class.

A simple query

A query is an expression that transforms sequences with one or more query operators. The simplest query comprises one input sequence and one operator. For instance, we can apply the Where operator on a simple array to extract those names whose length is at least four characters, as follows:

```
string[] names = { "Tom", "Dick", "Harry" };

IEnumerable<string> filteredNames =
  System.Linq.Enumerable.Where (
    names, n => n.Length >= 4);

foreach (string n in filteredNames)
  Console.Write (n + "|");                // Dick|Harry|
```

Because the standard query operators are implemented as extension methods, we can call Where directly on names, as though it were an instance method:

```
IEnumerable<string> filteredNames =
    names.Where (n => n.Length >= 4);
```

(For this to compile, you must import the System.Linq namespace with a using directive.) The Where method in System .Linq.Enumerable has the following signature:

```
static IEnumerable<TSource> Where<TSource> (
  this IEnumerable<TSource> source,
  Func<TSource,bool> predicate)
```

source is the *input sequence*; predicate is a delegate that is invoked on each input *element*. The Where method includes all elements in the *output sequence* for which the delegate returns true. Internally, it's implemented with an iterator—here's its source code:

```
foreach (TSource element in source)
  if (predicate (element))
    yield return element;
```

Projecting

Another fundamental query operator is the `Select` method. This transforms (*projects*) each element in the input sequence with a given lambda expression:

```
string[] names = { "Tom", "Dick", "Harry" };

IEnumerable<string> upperNames =
  names.Select (n => n.ToUpper());

foreach (string n in upperNames)
  Console.Write (n + "|");          // TOM|DICK|HARRY|
```

A query can project into an anonymous type:

```
var query = names.Select (n => new {
                                      Name = n,
                                      Length = n.Length
                                    });
foreach (var row in query)
  Console.WriteLine (row);
```

Here's the result:

```
{ Name = Tom, Length = 3 }
{ Name = Dick, Length = 4 }
{ Name = Harry, Length = 5 }
```

Take and Skip

The original ordering of elements within an input sequence is significant in LINQ. Some query operators rely on this behavior, such as `Take`, `Skip`, and `Reverse`. The `Take` operator outputs the first x elements, discarding the rest:

```
int[] numbers = { 10, 9, 8, 7, 6 };
IEnumerable<int> firstThree = numbers.Take (3);
// firstThree is { 10, 9, 8 }
```

The `Skip` operator ignores the first x elements, and outputs the rest:

```
IEnumerable<int> lastTwo = numbers.Skip (3);
```

Element operators

Not all query operators return a sequence. The *element* operators extract one element from the input sequence; examples are First, Last, Single, and ElementAt:

```
int[] numbers     = { 10, 9, 8, 7, 6 };
int firstNumber   = numbers.First();              // 10
int lastNumber    = numbers.Last();               // 6
int secondNumber  = numbers.ElementAt (2);        // 8
int firstOddNum   = numbers.First (n => n%2 == 1); // 9
```

All of these operators throw an exception if no elements are present. To avoid the exception, use FirstOrDefault, LastOrDefault, SingleOrDefault, or ElementAtOrDefault—these return null (or the default value for value types) when no element is found.

The Single and SingleOrDefault methods are equivalent to First and FirstOrDefault except that they throw an exception if there's more than one match. This behavior is useful when you're querying a database table for a row by primary key.

Aggregation operators

The *aggregation* operators return a scalar value, usually of numeric type. The most commonly used aggregation operators are Count, Min, Max, and Average:

```
int[] numbers = { 10, 9, 8, 7, 6 };
int count    = numbers.Count();       // 5
int min      = numbers.Min();         // 6
int max      = numbers.Max();         // 10
double avg   = numbers.Average();     // 8
```

Count accepts an optional predicate, which indicates whether to include a given element. The following counts all even numbers:

```
int evenNums = numbers.Count (n => n % 2 == 0);   // 3
```

The Min, Max, and Average operators accept an optional argument that transforms each element prior to it being aggregated:

```
int maxRemainderAfterDivBy5 = numbers.Max
                           (n => n % 5);        // 4
```

The following calculates the root-mean-square of numbers:

```
double rms = Math.Sqrt (numbers.Average (n => n * n));
```

Quantifiers

The *quantifiers* return a bool value. The quantifiers are Contains, Any, All, and SequenceEquals (which compares two sequences):

```
int[] numbers = { 10, 9, 8, 7, 6 };

bool hasTheNumberNine = numbers.Contains (9);       // true
bool hasMoreThanZeroElements = numbers.Any();       // true
bool hasOddNum = numbers.Any (n => n % 2 == 1);     // true
bool allOddNums = numbers.All (n => n % 2 == 1);    // false
```

Set operators

The *set* operators accept two same-typed input sequences. Concat appends one sequence to another; Union does the same but with duplicates removed:

```
int[] seq1 = { 1, 2, 3 }, seq2 = { 3, 4, 5 };

IEnumerable<int>
  concat = seq1.Concat (seq2),   // { 1, 2, 3, 3, 4, 5 }
  union  = seq1.Union  (seq2),   // { 1, 2, 3, 4, 5 }
```

The other two operators in this category are Intersect and Except:

```
IEnumerable<int>
  commonality = seq1.Intersect (seq2),   // { 3 }
  difference1 = seq1.Except    (seq2),   // { 1, 2 }
  difference2 = seq2.Except    (seq1);   // { 4, 5 }
```

Deferred Execution

An important feature of many query operators is that they execute not when constructed, but when *enumerated* (in other words, when MoveNext is called on its enumerator). Consider the following query:

```
var numbers = new List<int> { 1 };

IEnumerable<int> query = numbers.Select (n => n * 10);
numbers.Add (2);    // Sneak in an extra element

foreach (int n in query)
  Console.Write (n + "|");              // 10|20|
```

The extra number that we sneaked into the list *after* constructing the query is included in the result because it's not until the foreach statement runs that any filtering or sorting takes place. This is called *deferred* or *lazy* evaluation. Deferred execution decouples query *construction* from query *execution*, allowing you to construct a query in several steps, as well as making it possible to query a database without retrieving all the rows to the client. All standard query operators provide deferred execution, with the following exceptions:

- Operators that return a single element or scalar value (the *element operators*, *aggregation operators*, and *quantifiers*)

- The *conversion* operators ToArray, ToList, ToDictionary, ToLookup, and ToHashSet

The conversion operators are handy, in part because they defeat lazy evaluation. This can be useful to "freeze" or cache the results at a certain point in time, to avoid reexecuting a computationally intensive or remotely sourced query such as an Entity Framework table. (A side effect of lazy evaluation is that the query is reevaluated should you later reenumerate it.)

The following example illustrates the ToList operator:

```
var numbers = new List<int>() { 1, 2 };

List<int> timesTen = numbers
  .Select (n => n * 10)
  .ToList();    // Executes immediately into a List<int>

numbers.Clear();
Console.WriteLine (timesTen.Count);    // Still 2
```

NOTE

Subqueries provide another level of indirection. Everything in a subquery is subject to deferred execution, including aggregation and conversion methods, because the subquery is itself executed only lazily upon demand. Assuming names is a string array, a subquery looks like this:

```
names.Where (
  n => n.Length ==
    names.Min (n2 => n2.Length))
```

Standard Query Operators

We can divide the standard query operators (as implemented in the System.Linq.Enumerable class) into 12 categories, as summarized in Table 1.

Table 1. Query operator categories

Category	Description	Deferred execution?
Filtering	Returns a subset of elements that satisfy a given condition	Yes
Projecting	Transforms each element with a lambda function, optionally expanding subsequences	Yes
Joining	Meshes elements of one collection with another, using a time-efficient lookup strategy	Yes
Ordering	Returns a reordering of a sequence	Yes

Category	Description	Deferred execution?
Grouping	Groups a sequence into subsequences	Yes
Set	Accepts two same-typed sequences, and returns their commonality, sum, or difference	Yes
Element	Picks a single element from a sequence	No
Aggregation	Performs a computation over a sequence, returning a scalar value (typically a number)	No
Quantification	Performs a computation over a sequence, returning `true` or `false`	No
Conversion: Import	Converts a nongeneric sequence to a (queryable) generic sequence	Yes
Conversion: Export	Converts a sequence to an array, list, dictionary, or lookup, forcing immediate evaluation	No
Generation	Manufactures a simple sequence	Yes

Tables 2 through 13 summarize each query operator. The operators shown in bold have special support in C# (see "Query Expressions" on page 174).

Table 2. Filtering operators

Method	Description
Where	Returns a subset of elements that satisfy a given condition
Take	Returns the first *x* elements, and discards the rest
Skip	Ignores the first *x* elements, and returns the rest
TakeWhile	Emits elements from the input sequence until the given predicate is true
SkipWhile	Ignores elements from the input sequence until the given predicate is true and then emits the rest
Distinct	Returns a collection that excludes duplicates

Table 3. Projection operators

Method	Description
Select	Transforms each input element with a given lambda expression
SelectMany	Transforms each input element and then flattens and concatenates the resultant subsequences

Table 4. Joining operators

Method	Description
Join	Applies a lookup strategy to match elements from two collections, emitting a flat result set
GroupJoin	As above, but emits a *hierarchical* result set
Zip	Enumerates two sequences in step, returning a sequence that applies a function over each element pair

Table 5. Ordering operators

Method	Description
OrderBy, ThenBy	Returns the elements sorted in ascending order
OrderByDescending, ThenByDescending	Returns the elements sorted in descending order
Reverse	Returns the elements in reverse order

Table 6. Grouping operators

Method	Description
GroupBy	Groups a sequence into subsequences

Table 7. Set operators

Method	Description
Concat	Concatenates two sequences
Union	Concatenates two sequences, removing duplicates
Intersect	Returns elements present in both sequences
Except	Returns elements present in the first sequence, but not the second

Table 8. Element operators

Method	Description
First, FirstOrDefault	Returns the first element in the sequence, or the first element satisfying a given predicate
Last, LastOrDefault	Returns the last element in the sequence, or the last element satisfying a given predicate
Single, SingleOrDefault	Equivalent to First/FirstOrDefault, but throws an exception if there is more than one match
ElementAt, ElementAtOrDefault	Returns the element at the specified position
DefaultIfEmpty	Returns a single-value sequence whose value is null or default(TSource) if the sequence has no elements

Table 9. Aggregation operators

Method	Description
Count, LongCount	Returns the total number of elements in the input sequence, or the number of elements satisfying a given predicate
Min, Max	Returns the smallest or largest element in the sequence
Sum, Average	Calculates a numeric sum or average over elements in the sequence
Aggregate	Performs a custom aggregation

Table 10. Qualifiers

Method	Description
Contains	Returns true if the input sequence contains the given element
Any	Returns true if any elements satisfy the given predicate
All	Returns true if all elements satisfy the given predicate
SequenceEqual	Returns true if the second sequence has identical elements to the input sequence

Table 11. Conversion operators (import)

Method	Description
OfType	Converts IEnumerable to IEnumerable<T>, discarding wrongly typed elements
Cast	Converts IEnumerable to IEnumerable<T>, throwing an exception if there are any wrongly typed elements

Table 12. Conversion operators (export)

Method	Description
ToArray	Converts IEnumerable<T> to T[]
ToList	Converts IEnumerable<T> to List<T>

Method	Description
ToDictionary	Converts IEnumerable<T> to Dictionary<TKey,TValue>
ToHashSet	Converts IEnumerable<T> to HashSet<T>
ToLookup	Converts IEnumerable<T> to ILookup<TKey,TElement>
AsEnumerable	Downcasts to IEnumerable<T>
AsQueryable	Casts or converts to IQueryable<T>

Table 13. Generation operators

Method	Description
Empty	Creates an empty sequence
Repeat	Creates a sequence of repeating elements
Range	Creates a sequence of integers

Chaining Query Operators

To build more complex queries, you chain query operators together. For example, the following query extracts all strings containing the letter *a*, sorts them by length, and then converts the results to uppercase:

```
string[] names = { "Tom","Dick","Harry","Mary","Jay" };

IEnumerable<string> query = names
  .Where  (n => n.Contains ("a"))
  .OrderBy (n => n.Length)
  .Select  (n => n.ToUpper());

foreach (string name in query)
  Console.Write (name + "|");

// RESULT: JAY|MARY|HARRY|
```

Where, OrderBy, and Select are all standard query operators that resolve to extension methods in the Enumerable class. The Where operator emits a filtered version of the input sequence;

OrderBy emits a sorted version of its input sequence; Select emits a sequence in which each input element is transformed or *projected* with a given lambda expression (n.ToUpper(), in this case). Data flows from left to right through the chain of operators, so the data is first filtered, then sorted, then projected. The end result resembles a production line of conveyor belts, as illustrated in Figure 6.

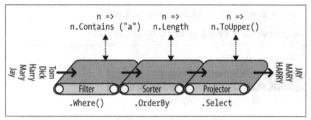

Figure 6. Chaining query operators

Deferred execution is honored throughout with operators, so no filtering, sorting, or projecting takes place until the query is actually enumerated.

Query Expressions

So far, we've written queries by calling extension methods in the Enumerable class. In this book, we describe this as *fluent syntax*. C# also provides special language support for writing queries, called *query expressions*. Here's the preceding query expressed as a query expression:

```
IEnumerable<string> query =
  from n in names
  where n.Contains ("a")
  orderby n.Length
  select n.ToUpper();
```

A query expression always starts with a from clause, and ends with either a select or group clause. The from clause declares a *range variable* (in this case, n), which you can think of as traversing the input collection—rather like foreach. Figure 7 illustrates the complete syntax.

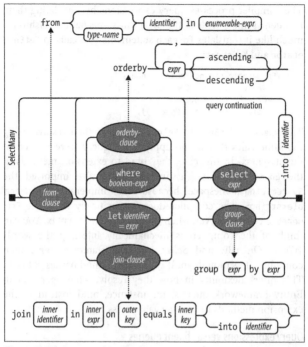

Figure 7. Query expression syntax

NOTE

If you're familiar with SQL, LINQ's query expression syntax—with the `from` clause first and the `select` clause last—might look bizarre. Query expression syntax is actually more logical because the clauses appear *in the order they're executed*. This allows Visual Studio to prompt you with IntelliSense as you type as well as simplifying the scoping rules for subqueries.

The compiler processes query expressions by translating them to fluent syntax. It does this in a fairly mechanical fashion—much like it translates `foreach` statements into calls to `GetEnumerator` and `MoveNext`:

```
IEnumerable<string> query = names
  .Where   (n => n.Contains ("a"))
  .OrderBy (n => n.Length)
  .Select  (n => n.ToUpper());
```

The `Where`, `OrderBy`, and `Select` operators then resolve using the same rules that would apply if the query were written in fluent syntax. In this case, they bind to extension methods in the `Enumerable` class (assuming that you've imported the `System.Linq` namespace) because `names` implements `IEnumerable<string>`. The compiler doesn't specifically favor the `Enumerable` class, however, when translating query syntax. You can think of the compiler as mechanically injecting the words *Where*, *OrderBy*, and *Select* into the statement, and then compiling it as though you'd typed the method names yourself. This offers flexibility in how they resolve—the operators in Entity Framework queries, for instance, bind instead to the extension methods in the `Queryable` class.

Query expressions versus fluent queries

Query expressions and fluent queries each have advantages.

Query expressions support only a small subset of query operators, namely:

```
Where, Select, SelectMany
OrderBy, ThenBy, OrderByDescending, ThenByDescending
GroupBy, Join, GroupJoin
```

For queries that use other operators, you must either write entirely in fluent syntax or construct mixed-syntax queries; for example:

```
string[] names = { "Tom","Dick","Harry","Mary","Jay" };

IEnumerable<string> query =
  from  n in names
```

```
    where  n.Length == names.Min (n2 => n2.Length)
    select n;
```

This query returns names whose length matches that of the shortest names ("Tom" and "Jay"). The subquery (in bold) calculates the minimum length of each name and evaluates to 3. We need to use fluent syntax for the subquery, because the Min operator has no support in query expression syntax. We can, however, still use query syntax for the outer query.

The main advantage of query syntax is that it can radically simplify queries that involve the following:

- A let clause for introducing a new variable alongside the range variable
- Multiple generators (SelectMany) followed by an outer range variable reference
- A Join or GroupJoin equivalent, followed by an outer range variable reference

The let Keyword

The let keyword introduces a new variable alongside the range variable. For instance, suppose that you want to list all names whose length, without vowels, is greater than two characters:

```
string[] names = { "Tom","Dick","Harry","Mary","Jay" };

IEnumerable<string> query =
  from n in names
  let vowelless = Regex.Replace (n, "[aeiou]", "")
  where vowelless.Length > 2
  orderby vowelless
  select n + " - " + vowelless;
```

The output from enumerating this query is:

```
Dick - Dck
Harry - Hrry
Mary - Mry
```

The let clause performs a calculation on each element, without losing the original element. In our query, the subsequent clauses (where, orderby, and select) have access to both n and vowelless. A query can include multiple let clauses, and they can be interspersed with additional where and join clauses.

The compiler translates the let keyword by projecting into a temporary anonymous type that contains both the original and transformed elements:

```
IEnumerable<string> query = names
  .Select (n => new
    {
      n = n,
      vowelless = Regex.Replace (n, "[aeiou]", "")
    }
  )
  .Where (temp0 => (temp0.vowelless.Length > 2))
  .OrderBy (temp0 => temp0.vowelless)
  .Select (temp0 => ((temp0.n + " - ") + temp0.vowelless))
```

Query Continuations

If you want to add clauses *after* a select or group clause, you must use the into keyword to "continue" the query. For instance:

```
from c in "The quick brown tiger".Split()
select c.ToUpper() into upper
where upper.StartsWith ("T")
select upper

// RESULT: "THE", "TIGER"
```

Following an into clause, the previous range variable is out of scope.

The compiler translates queries with an into keyword simply into a longer chain of operators:

```
"The quick brown tiger".Split()
  .Select (c => c.ToUpper())
  .Where (upper => upper.StartsWith ("T"))
```

(It omits the final Select(upper=>upper) because it's redundant.)

Multiple Generators

A query can include multiple generators (from clauses). For example:

```
int[] numbers = { 1, 2, 3 };
string[] letters = { "a", "b" };

IEnumerable<string> query = from n in numbers
                            from l in letters
                            select n.ToString() + l;
```

The result is a cross product, rather like you'd get with nested foreach loops:

```
"1a", "1b", "2a", "2b", "3a", "3b"
```

When there's more than one from clause in a query, the compiler emits a call to SelectMany:

```
IEnumerable<string> query = numbers.SelectMany (
    n => letters,
    (n, l) => (n.ToString() + l));
```

SelectMany performs nested looping. It enumerates every element in the source collection (numbers), transforming each element with the first lambda expression (letters). This generates a sequence of *subsequences*, which it then enumerates. The final output elements are determined by the second lambda expression (n.ToString()+l).

If you subsequently apply a where clause, you can filter the cross product and project a result akin to a *join*:

```
string[] players = { "Tom", "Jay", "Mary" };

IEnumerable<string> query =
  from name1 in players
  from name2 in players
  where name1.CompareTo (name2) < 0
  orderby name1, name2
  select name1 + " vs " + name2;
```

```
RESULT: { "Jay vs Mary", "Jay vs Tom", "Mary vs Tom" }
```

The translation of this query into fluent syntax is more complex, requiring a temporary anonymous projection. The ability to perform this translation automatically is one of the key benefits of query expressions.

The expression in the second generator is allowed to use the first range variable:

```
string[] fullNames =
  { "Anne Williams", "John Fred Smith", "Sue Green" };

IEnumerable<string> query =
  from fullName in fullNames
  from name in fullName.Split()
  select name + " came from " + fullName;

Anne came from Anne Williams
Williams came from Anne Williams
John came from John Fred Smith
```

This works because the expression fullName.Split emits a *sequence* (an array of strings).

Multiple generators are used extensively in database queries, to flatten parent-child relationships and to perform manual joins.

Joining

LINQ provides three *joining* operators, the main ones being Join and GroupJoin, which perform keyed lookup-based joins. Join and GroupJoin support only a subset of the functionality you get with multiple generators/SelectMany, but are more performant with local queries because they use a hashtable-based lookup strategy rather than performing nested loops. (With Entity Framework queries, the joining operators have no advantage over multiple generators.)

Join and GroupJoin support only *equi-joins* (i.e., the joining condition must use the equality operator). There are two

---

methods: `Join` and `GroupJoin`. `Join` emits a flat result set, whereas `GroupJoin` emits a hierarchical result set.

Following is the query expression syntax for a flat join:

```
from outer-var in outer-sequence
join inner-var in inner-sequence
  on outer-key-expr equals inner-key-expr
```

For example, given the following collections

```
var customers = new[]
{
  new { ID = 1, Name = "Tom" },
  new { ID = 2, Name = "Dick" },
  new { ID = 3, Name = "Harry" }
};
var purchases = new[]
{
  new { CustomerID = 1, Product = "House" },
  new { CustomerID = 2, Product = "Boat" },
  new { CustomerID = 2, Product = "Car" },
  new { CustomerID = 3, Product = "Holiday" }
};
```

we could perform a join as follows:

```
IEnumerable<string> query =
  from c in customers
  join p in purchases on c.ID equals p.CustomerID
  select c.Name + " bought a " + p.Product;
```

The compiler translates this to:

```
customers.Join (                  // outer collection
  purchases,                      // inner collection
  c => c.ID,                      // outer key selector
  p => p.CustomerID,              // inner key selector
  (c, p) =>                       // result selector
    c.Name + " bought a " + p.Product
);
```

Here's the result:

```
Tom bought a House
Dick bought a Boat
Dick bought a Car
Harry bought a Holiday
```

With local sequences, `Join` and `GroupJoin` are more efficient at processing large collections than `SelectMany` because they first preload the inner sequence into a keyed hashtable-based lookup. With a database query, however, you could achieve the same result equally efficiently as follows:

```
from c in customers
from p in purchases
where c.ID == p.CustomerID
select c.Name + " bought a " + p.Product;
```

GroupJoin

`GroupJoin` does the same work as `Join`, but instead of yielding a flat result, it yields a hierarchical result, grouped by each outer element.

The query expression syntax for `GroupJoin` is the same as for `Join`, but is followed by the `into` keyword. Here's a basic example, using the `customers` and `purchases` collections we set up in the previous section:

```
IEnumerable<IEnumerable<Purchase>> query =
  from c in customers
  join p in purchases on c.ID equals p.CustomerID
  into custPurchases
  select custPurchases;   // custPurchases is a sequence
```

NOTE

An `into` clause translates to `GroupJoin` only when it appears directly after a `join` clause. After a `select` or `group` clause it means *query continuation*. The two uses of the `into` keyword are quite different, although they have one feature in common: they both introduce a new query variable.

The result is a sequence of sequences, which you could enumerate as follows:

```
foreach (IEnumerable<Purchase> purchaseSequence in query)
  foreach (Purchase p in purchaseSequence)
    Console.WriteLine (p.Description);
```

This isn't very useful, however, because outerSeq has no reference to the outer customer. More commonly, you'd reference
the outer range variable in the projection:

```
from c in customers
join p in purchases on c.ID equals p.CustomerID
into custPurchases
select new { CustName = c.Name, custPurchases };
```

You could obtain the same result (but less efficiently, for local
queries) by projecting into an anonymous type that included a
subquery:

```
from c in customers
select new
{
  CustName = c.Name,
  custPurchases =
    purchases.Where (p => c.ID == p.CustomerID)
}
```

Zip

Zip is the simplest joining operator. It enumerates two sequences in step (like a zipper), returning a sequence based on applying a function over each element pair; thus

```
int[] numbers = { 3, 5, 7 };
string[] words = { "three", "five", "seven", "ignored" };
IEnumerable<string> zip =
  numbers.Zip (words, (n, w) => n + "=" + w);
```

produces a sequence with the following elements:

```
3=three
5=five
7=seven
```

Extra elements in either input sequence are ignored. Zip is not
supported when you are querying a database.

Ordering

The `orderby` keyword sorts a sequence. You can specify any number of expressions upon which to sort:

```
string[] names = { "Tom","Dick","Harry","Mary","Jay" };

IEnumerable<string> query = from n in names
                            orderby n.Length, n
                            select n;
```

This sorts first by length and then by name, yielding this result:

```
Jay, Tom, Dick, Mary, Harry
```

The compiler translates the first `orderby` expression to a call to `OrderBy`, and subsequent expressions to a call to `ThenBy`:

```
IEnumerable<string> query = names
    .OrderBy (n => n.Length)
    .ThenBy (n => n)
```

The `ThenBy` operator *refines* rather than *replaces* the previous sorting.

You can include the `descending` keyword after any of the `orderby` expressions:

```
orderby n.Length descending, n
```

This translates to the following:

```
.OrderByDescending (n => n.Length).ThenBy (n => n)
```

NOTE

The ordering operators return an extended type of `IEnumerable<T>` called `IOrderedEnumerable<T>`. This interface defines the extra functionality required by the `ThenBy` operator.

Grouping

GroupBy organizes a flat input sequence into sequences of *groups*. For example, the following groups a sequence of names by their length:

```
string[] names = { "Tom","Dick","Harry","Mary","Jay" };

var query = from name in names
            group name by name.Length;
```

The compiler translates this query into the following:

```
IEnumerable<IGrouping<int,string>> query =
    names.GroupBy (name => name.Length);
```

Here's how to enumerate the result:

```
foreach (IGrouping<int,string> grouping in query)
{
  Console.Write ("\r\n Length=" + grouping.Key + ":");
  foreach (string name in grouping)
    Console.Write (" " + name);
}

  Length=3: Tom Jay
  Length=4: Dick Mary
  Length=5: Harry
```

Enumerable.GroupBy works by reading the input elements into a temporary dictionary of lists so that all elements with the same key end up in the same sublist. It then emits a sequence of *groupings*. A grouping is a sequence with a Key property:

```
public interface IGrouping <TKey,TElement>
  : IEnumerable<TElement>, IEnumerable
{
  // Key applies to the subsequence as a whole
  TKey Key { get; }
}
```

By default, the elements in each grouping are untransformed input elements, unless you specify an elementSelector argument. The following projects each input element to uppercase:

```
from name in names
group name.ToUpper() by name.Length
```

which translates to this:

```
names.GroupBy (
   name => name.Length,
   name => name.ToUpper() )
```

The subcollections are not emitted in order of key. GroupBy does no *sorting* (in fact, it preserves the original ordering). To sort, you must add an OrderBy operator (which means first adding an into clause, because group by ordinarily ends a query):

```
from name in names
group name.ToUpper() by name.Length into grouping
orderby grouping.Key
select grouping
```

Query continuations are often used in a group by query. The next query filters out groups that have exactly two matches in them:

```
from name in names
group name.ToUpper() by name.Length into grouping
where grouping.Count() == 2
select grouping
```

NOTE

A where after a group by is equivalent to HAVING in SQL. It applies to each subsequence or grouping as a whole rather than the individual elements.

OfType and Cast

OfType and Cast accept a nongeneric IEnumerable collection and emit a generic IEnumerable<T> sequence that you can subsequently query:

```
var classicList = new System.Collections.ArrayList();
classicList.AddRange ( new int[] { 3, 4, 5 } );
IEnumerable<int> sequence1 = classicList.Cast<int>();
```

This is useful because it allows you to query collections written prior to C# 2.0 (when IEnumerable<T> was introduced), such as ControlCollection in System.Windows.Forms.

Cast and OfType differ in their behavior when encountering an input element that's of an incompatible type: Cast throws an exception, whereas OfType ignores the incompatible element.

The rules for element compatibility follow those of C#'s is operator. Here's the internal implementation of Cast:

```
public static IEnumerable<TSource> Cast <TSource>
               (IEnumerable source)
{
   foreach (object element in source)
     yield return (TSource)element;
}
```

C# supports the Cast operator in query expressions—simply insert the element type immediately after the from keyword:

```
from int x in classicList ...
```

This translates to the following:

```
from x in classicList.Cast <int>() ...
```

Dynamic Binding

Dynamic binding defers *binding*—the process of resolving types, members, and operations—from compile time to runtime. Dynamic binding is useful when at compile time *you* know that a certain function, member, or operation exists, but the *compiler* does not. This commonly occurs when you are interoperating with dynamic languages (such as IronPython) and COM and in scenarios when you might otherwise use reflection.

A dynamic type is declared by using the contextual keyword dynamic:

```
dynamic d = GetSomeObject();
d.Quack();
```

A dynamic type instructs the compiler to relax. We expect the runtime type of d to have a Quack method. We just can't prove it statically. Because d is dynamic, the compiler defers binding Quack to d until runtime. Understanding what this means requires distinguishing between *static binding* and *dynamic binding*.

Static Binding versus Dynamic Binding

The canonical binding example is mapping a name to a specific function when compiling an expression. To compile the following expression, the compiler needs to find the implementation of the method named Quack:

```
d.Quack();
```

Let's suppose the static type of d is Duck:

```
Duck d = ...
d.Quack();
```

In the simplest case, the compiler does the binding by looking for a parameterless method named Quack on Duck. Failing that, the compiler extends its search to methods taking optional parameters, methods on base classes of Duck, and extension methods that take Duck as its first parameter. If no match is found, you'll get a compilation error. Regardless of what method is bound, the bottom line is that the binding is done by the compiler, and the binding utterly depends on statically knowing the types of the operands (in this case, d). This makes it *static binding*.

Now let's change the static type of d to object:

```
object d = ...
d.Quack();
```

Calling Quack gives us a compilation error because although the value stored in d can contain a method called Quack, the compiler cannot know it given that the only information it has is the type of the variable, which in this case is object. But let's now change the static type of d to dynamic:

```
dynamic d = ...
d.Quack();
```

A dynamic type is like object—it's equally nondescriptive about a type. The difference is that it lets you use it in ways that aren't known at compile time. A dynamic object binds at runtime based on its runtime type, not its compile-time type. When the compiler sees a dynamically bound expression (which in general is an expression that contains any value of type dynamic), it merely packages up the expression such that the binding can be done later at runtime.

At runtime, if a dynamic object implements IDynamicMetaOb jectProvider, that interface is used to perform the binding. If not, binding occurs in almost the same way as it would have had the compiler known the dynamic object's runtime type. These two alternatives are called *custom binding* and *language binding*.

Custom Binding

Custom binding occurs when a dynamic object implements IDy namicMetaObjectProvider (IDMOP). Although you can implement IDMOP on types that you write in C#, and this is useful to do, the more common case is that you have acquired an IDMOP object from a dynamic language that is implemented in .NET on the Dynamic Language Runtime (DLR), such as IronPython or IronRuby. Objects from those languages implicitly implement IDMOP as a means to directly control the meanings of operations performed on them. Here's a simple example:

```
using System;
using System.Dynamic;

public class Test
{
  static void Main()
  {
    dynamic d = new Duck();
    d.Quack();       // Quack was called
```

```
    d.Waddle();      // Waddle was called
  }
}
public class Duck : DynamicObject
{
  public override bool TryInvokeMember (
    InvokeMemberBinder binder, object[] args,
    out object result)
  {
    Console.WriteLine (binder.Name + " was called");
    result = null;
    return true;
  }
}
```

The Duck class doesn't actually have a Quack method. Instead, it uses custom binding to intercept and interpret all method calls.

We discuss custom binders in greater detail in Chapter 20 of *C# 8.0 in a Nutshell*.

Language Binding

Language binding occurs when a dynamic object does not implement IDynamicMetaObjectProvider. Language binding is useful when you are working around imperfectly designed types or inherent limitations in the .NET type system. For example, the built-in numeric types are imperfect in that they have no common interface. We have seen that methods can be bound dynamically; the same is true for operators:

```
static dynamic Mean (dynamic x, dynamic y) => (x+y) / 2;

static void Main()
{
  int x = 3, y = 4;
  Console.WriteLine (Mean (x, y));
}
```

The benefit is obvious—you don't need to duplicate code for each numeric type. However, you lose static type safety, risking runtime exceptions rather than compile-time errors.

Dynamic binding circumvents static type safety but not runtime type safety. Unlike with reflection, you cannot circumvent member accessibility rules with dynamic binding.

By design, language runtime binding behaves as similarly as possible to static binding, had the runtime types of the dynamic objects been known at compile time. In the previous example, the behavior of our program would be identical if we hardcoded Mean to work with the int type. The most notable exception in parity between static and dynamic binding is for extension methods, which we discuss in "Uncallable Functions" on page 195.

NOTE

Dynamic binding also incurs a performance hit. Because of the DLR's caching mechanisms, however, repeated calls to the same dynamic expression are optimized, allowing you to efficiently call dynamic expressions in a loop. This optimization brings the typical overhead for a simple dynamic expression on today's hardware down to less than 100 ns.

RuntimeBinderException

If a member fails to bind, a RuntimeBinderException is thrown. You can think of this like a compile-time error at runtime:

```
dynamic d = 5;
d.Hello();       // throws RuntimeBinderException
```

The exception is thrown because the int type has no Hello method.

Runtime Representation of dynamic

There is a deep equivalence between the dynamic and object types. The runtime treats the following expression as true:

```
typeof (dynamic) == typeof (object)
```

This principle extends to constructed types and array types:

```
typeof (List<dynamic>) == typeof (List<object>)
typeof (dynamic[]) == typeof (object[])
```

Like an object reference, a dynamic reference can point to an object of any type (except pointer types):

```
dynamic x = "hello";
Console.WriteLine (x.GetType().Name);  // String

x = 123;  // No error (despite same variable)
Console.WriteLine (x.GetType().Name);  // Int32
```

Structurally, there is no difference between an object reference and a dynamic reference. A dynamic reference simply enables dynamic operations on the object it points to. You can convert from object to dynamic to perform any dynamic operation you want on an object:

```
object o = new System.Text.StringBuilder();
dynamic d = o;
d.Append ("hello");
Console.WriteLine (o);  // hello
```

Dynamic Conversions

The dynamic type has implicit conversions to and from all other types. For a conversion to succeed, the runtime type of the dynamic object must be implicitly convertible to the target static type.

The following example throws a RuntimeBinderException because an int is not implicitly convertible to a short:

```
int i = 7;
dynamic d = i;
long l = d;      // OK - implicit conversion works
short j = d;     // throws RuntimeBinderException
```

---

var versus dynamic

The var and dynamic types bear a superficial resemblance, but the difference is deep:

var says, "Let the *compiler* figure out the type."

dynamic says, "Let the *runtime* figure out the type."

To illustrate:

```
dynamic x = "hello";   // Static type is dynamic
var y = "hello";       // Static type is string
int i = x;             // Runtime error
int j = y;             // Compile-time error
```

Dynamic Expressions

Fields, properties, methods, events, constructors, indexers, operators, and conversions can all be called dynamically.

Trying to consume the result of a dynamic expression with a void return type is prohibited—just as with a statically typed expression. The difference is that the error occurs at runtime.

Expressions involving dynamic operands are typically themselves dynamic, since the effect of absent type information is cascading:

```
dynamic x = 2;
var y = x * 3;         // Static type of y is dynamic
```

There are a couple of obvious exceptions to this rule. First, casting a dynamic expression to a static type yields a static expression. Second, constructor invocations always yield static expressions—even when called with dynamic arguments.

In addition, there are a few edge cases for which an expression containing a dynamic argument is static, including passing an index to an array and delegating creation expressions.

Dynamic Member Overload Resolution

The canonical use case for dynamic involves a dynamic *receiver*. This means that a dynamic object is the receiver of a dynamic function call:

```
dynamic x = ...;
x.Foo (123);          // x is the receiver
```

However, dynamic binding is not limited to receivers: the method arguments are also eligible for dynamic binding. The effect of calling a function with dynamic arguments is to defer overload resolution from compile-time to runtime:

```
static void Foo (int x)    => Console.WriteLine ("int");
static void Foo (string x) => Console.WriteLine ("str");

static void Main()
{
  dynamic x = 5;
  dynamic y = "watermelon";

  Foo (x);    // 1
  Foo (y);    // 2
}
```

Runtime overload resolution is also called *multiple dispatch* and is useful in implementing design patterns such as *visitor*.

If a dynamic receiver is not involved, the compiler can statically perform a basic check to see whether the dynamic call will succeed: it checks that a function with the right name and number of parameters exists. If no candidate is found, you get a compile-time error.

If a function is called with a mixture of dynamic and static arguments, the final choice of method will reflect a mixture of dynamic and static binding decisions:

```
static void X(object x, object y) =>Console.Write("oo");
static void X(object x, string y) =>Console.Write("os");
static void X(string x, object y) =>Console.Write("so");
static void X(string x, string y) =>Console.Write("ss");

static void Main()
```

```
{
  object o = "hello";
  dynamic d = "goodbye";
  X (o, d);                // os
}
```

The call to X(o,d) is dynamically bound because one of its arguments, d, is dynamic. But because o is statically known, the binding—even though it occurs dynamically—will make use of that. In this case, overload resolution will pick the second implementation of X due to the static type of o and the runtime type of d. In other words, the compiler is "as static as it can possibly be."

Uncallable Functions

Some functions cannot be called dynamically. You cannot call the following:

- Extension methods (via extension method syntax)
- Any member of an interface (via the interface)
- Base members hidden by a subclass

This is because dynamic binding requires two pieces of information: the name of the function to call, and the object upon which to call the function. However, in each of the three uncallable scenarios, an *additional type* is involved, which is known only at compile time. And there is no way to specify these additional types dynamically.

When you are calling extension methods, that additional type is an extension class, chosen implicitly by virtue of using directives in your source code (which disappear after compilation). When calling members via an interface, you communicate the additional type via an implicit or explicit cast. (With explicit implementation, it's in fact impossible to call a member without casting to the interface.) A similar situation arises when you are calling a hidden base member: you must specify an additional type via either a cast or the base keyword—and that additional type is lost at runtime.

Operator Overloading

You can overload operators to provide more natural syntax for custom types. Operator overloading is most appropriately used for implementing custom structs that represent fairly primitive data types. For example, a custom numeric type is an excellent candidate for operator overloading.

You can overload the following symbolic operators:

```
+    -    *    /    ++    --    !    ~    %    &    |    ^
==   !=   <    <<   >>    >
```

You can override implicit and explicit conversions (with the implicit and explicit keywords), as you can the true and false operators.

The compound assignment operators (e.g., +=, /=) are automatically overridden when you override the noncompound operators (e.g., +, /).

Operator Functions

To overload an operator, you declare an *operator function*. An operator function must be static, and at least one of the operands must be the type in which the operator function is declared.

In the following example, we define a struct called Note, representing a musical note, and then overload the + operator:

```
public struct Note
{
  int value;

  public Note (int semitonesFromA)
    => value = semitonesFromA;

  public static Note operator + (Note x, int semitones)
  {
```

```
        return new Note (x.value + semitones);
    }
}
```

This overload allows us to add an int to a Note:

```
Note B = new Note (2);
Note CSharp = B + 2;
```

Because we overrode +, we can use +=, too:

```
CSharp += 2;
```

Just as with methods and properties, C# 6 and later allow operator functions comprising a single expression to be written more tersely with expression-bodied syntax:

```
public static Note operator + (Note x, int semitones)
  => new Note (x.value + semitones);
```

Overloading Equality and Comparison Operators

Equality and comparison operators are often overridden when writing structs, and in rare cases with classes. Special rules and obligations apply, when overloading these operators:

Pairing
> The C# compiler enforces that operators that are logical pairs are both defined. These operators are (== !=), (< >), and (<= >=).

Equals *and* GetHashCode
> If you overload == and !=, you will usually need to override object's Equals and GetHashCode methods so that collections and hashtables will work reliably with the type.

IComparable *and* IComparable<T>
> If you overload < and >, you would also typically implement IComparable and IComparable<T>.

Extending the previous example, here's how you could overload Note's equality operators:

```
public static bool operator == (Note n1, Note n2)
  => n1.value == n2.value;
```

```csharp
public static bool operator != (Note n1, Note n2)
  => !(n1.value == n2.value);

public override bool Equals (object otherNote)
{
  if (!(otherNote is Note)) return false;
  return this == (Note)otherNote;
}
// value's hashcode will work for our own hashcode:
public override int GetHashCode() => value.GetHashCode();
```

Custom Implicit and Explicit Conversions

Implicit and explicit conversions are overloadable operators.
These conversions are typically overloaded to make converting
between strongly related types (such as numeric types) concise
and natural.

As explained in the discussion on types, the rationale behind
implicit conversions is that they should always succeed and not
lose information during conversion. Otherwise, explicit conversions should be defined.

In the following example, we define conversions between our
musical Note type and a double (which represents the fre-
quency in hertz of that note):

```csharp
...
// Convert to hertz
public static implicit operator double (Note x)
  => 440 * Math.Pow (2,(double) x.value / 12 );

// Convert from hertz (accurate to nearest semitone)
public static explicit operator Note (double x)
  => new Note ((int) (0.5 + 12 * (Math.Log(x/440)
                     / Math.Log(2)) ));
...

Note n =(Note)554.37;   // explicit conversion
double x = n;           // implicit conversion
```

This example is somewhat contrived: in real life, these conversions might be better implemented with a ToFrequency method and a (static) FromFrequency method.

Custom conversions are ignored by the as and is operators.

Attributes

You're already familiar with the notion of attributing code elements of a program with modifiers, such as virtual or ref. These constructs are built into the language. *Attributes* are an extensible mechanism for adding custom information to code elements (assemblies, types, members, return values, and parameters). This extensibility is useful for services that integrate deeply into the type system, without requiring special keywords or constructs in the C# language.

A good scenario for attributes is *serialization*—the process of converting arbitrary objects to and from a particular format for storage or transmission. In this scenario, an attribute on a field can specify the translation between C#'s representation of the field and the format's representation of the field.

Attribute Classes

An attribute is defined by a class that inherits (directly or indirectly) from the abstract class System.Attribute. To attach an attribute to a code element, specify the attribute's type name in square brackets, before the code element. For example, the following attaches the ObsoleteAttribute to the Foo class:

```
[ObsoleteAttribute]
public class Foo {...}
```

This particular attribute is recognized by the compiler and will cause compiler warnings if a type or member marked obsolete is referenced. By convention, all attribute types end with the word *Attribute*. C# recognizes this and allows you to omit the suffix when attaching an attribute:

```
[Obsolete]
public class Foo {...}
```

ObsoleteAttribute is a type declared in the System namespace as follows (simplified for brevity):

```
public sealed class ObsoleteAttribute : Attribute {...}
```

Named and Positional Attribute Parameters

Attributes can have parameters. In the following example, we apply XmlElementAttribute to a class. This attribute instructs XmlSerializer (in System.Xml.Serialization) how an object is represented in XML and accepts several *attribute parameters*. The following attribute maps the CustomerEntity class to an XML element named Customer, belonging to the http://oreilly.com namespace:

```
[XmlElement ("Customer", Namespace="http://oreilly.com")]
public class CustomerEntity { ... }
```

Attribute parameters fall into one of two categories: positional or named. In the preceding example, the first argument is a *positional parameter*; the second is a *named parameter*. Positional parameters correspond to parameters of the attribute type's public constructors. Named parameters correspond to public fields or public properties on the attribute type.

When specifying an attribute, you must include positional parameters that correspond to one of the attribute's constructors. Named parameters are optional.

Attribute Targets

Implicitly, the target of an attribute is the code element it immediately precedes, which is typically a type or type member. You can also attach attributes, however, to an assembly. This requires that you explicitly specify the attribute's target. Here's an example of using the CLSCompliant attribute to specify Common Language Specification (CLS) compliance for an entire assembly:

```
[assembly:CLSCompliant(true)]
```

Specifying Multiple Attributes

You can specify multiple attributes for a single code element. You can list each attribute either within the same pair of square brackets (separated by a comma) or in separate pairs of square brackets (or a combination of the two). The following two examples are semantically identical:

```
[Serializable, Obsolete, CLSCompliant(false)]
public class Bar {...}

[Serializable] [Obsolete] [CLSCompliant(false)]
public class Bar {...}
```

Writing Custom Attributes

You can define your own attributes by subclassing Sys tem.Attribute. For example, you could use the following custom attribute for flagging a method for unit testing:

```
[AttributeUsage (AttributeTargets.Method)]
public sealed class TestAttribute : Attribute
{
  public int      Repetitions;
  public string   FailureMessage;

  public TestAttribute () : this (1) { }
  public TestAttribute (int repetitions)
    => Repetitions = repetitions;
}
```

Here's how you could apply the attribute:

```
class Foo
{
  [Test]
  public void Method1() { ... }

  [Test(20)]
  public void Method2() { ... }
```

```
    [Test(20, FailureMessage="Debugging Time!")]
    public void Method3() { ... }
}
```

AttributeUsage is itself an attribute that indicates the construct (or combination of constructs) to which the custom attribute can be applied. The AttributeTargets enum includes such members as Class, Method, Parameter, and Constructor (as well as All, which combines all targets).

Retrieving Attributes at Runtime

There are two standard ways to retrieve attributes at runtime:

- Call GetCustomAttributes on any Type or MemberInfo object

- Call Attribute.GetCustomAttribute or Attribute.GetCustomAttributes

These latter two methods are overloaded to accept any reflection object that corresponds to a valid attribute target (Type, Assembly, Module, MemberInfo, or ParameterInfo).

Here's how we can enumerate each method in the preceding Foo class that has a TestAttribute:

```
foreach (MethodInfo mi in typeof (Foo).GetMethods())
{
  TestAttribute att = (TestAttribute)
    Attribute.GetCustomAttribute
     (mi, typeof (TestAttribute));

  if (att != null)
    Console.WriteLine (
      "{0} will be tested; reps={1}; msg={2}",
      mi.Name, att.Repetitions, att.FailureMessage);
}
```

Here's the output:

```
Method1 will be tested; reps=1; msg=
Method2 will be tested; reps=20; msg=
Method3 will be tested; reps=20; msg=Debugging Time!
```

Caller Info Attributes

From C# 5.0, you can tag optional parameters with one of three *caller info attributes*, which instruct the compiler to feed information obtained from the caller's source code into the parameter's default value:

- [CallerMemberName] applies the caller's member name.
- [CallerFilePath] applies the path to the caller's source code file.
- [CallerLineNumber] applies the line number in the caller's source code file.

The Foo method in the following program demonstrates all three:

```
using System;
using System.Runtime.CompilerServices;

class Program
{
  static void Main() => Foo();

  static void Foo (
    [CallerMemberName] string memberName = null,
    [CallerFilePath] string filePath = null,
    [CallerLineNumber] int lineNumber = 0)
  {
    Console.WriteLine (memberName);
    Console.WriteLine (filePath);
    Console.WriteLine (lineNumber);
  }
}
```

Assuming that our program resides in *c:\source\test\Program.cs*, the output would be:

```
Main
c:\source\test\Program.cs
6
```

As with standard optional parameters, the substitution is done at the *calling site*. Hence, our Main method is syntactic sugar for this:

```
static void Main()
    => Foo ("Main", @"c:\source\test\Program.cs", 6);
```

Caller info attributes are useful for writing logging functions and for implementing change notification patterns. For instance, we can call a method such as the following from within a property's set accessor—without having to specify the property's name:

```
void RaisePropertyChanged (
  [CallerMemberName] string propertyName = null)
  {
    ...
  }
```

Asynchronous Functions

The await and async keywords (introduced in C# 5) support *asynchronous programming*, a style of programming in which long-running functions do most or all of their work *after* returning to the caller. This is in contrast to normal *synchronous* programming in which long-running functions *block* the caller until the operation is complete. Asynchronous programming implies *concurrency* because the long-running operation continues *in parallel* to the caller. The implementer of an asynchronous function initiates this concurrency either through multithreading (for compute-bound operations) or via a callback mechanism (for I/O-bound operations).

Multithreading, concurrency, and asynchronous programming are large topics. We dedicate two chapters to them in *C# 8.0 in a Nutshell*, and discuss them online at *http://alba hari.com/threading*.

For instance, consider the following *synchronous* method, which is long-running and compute-bound:

```
int ComplexCalculation()
{
  double x = 2;
  for (int i = 1; i < 100000000; i++)
    x += Math.Sqrt (x) / i;
  return (int)x;
}
```

This method blocks the caller for a few seconds while it runs, before returning the result of the calculation to the caller:

```
int result = ComplexCalculation();
// Sometime later:
Console.WriteLine (result);   // 116
```

The CLR defines a class called Task<TResult> (in System .Threading.Tasks) to encapsulate the concept of an operation that completes in the future. You can generate a Task<TResult> for a compute-bound operation by calling Task.Run, which instructs the CLR to run the specified delegate on a separate thread that executes in parallel to the caller:

```
Task<int> ComplexCalculationAsync()
{
  return Task.Run (() => ComplexCalculation());
}
```

This method is *asynchronous* because it returns immediately to the caller while it executes concurrently. However, we need some mechanism to allow the caller to specify what should happen when the operation finishes and the result becomes available. `Task<TResult>` solves this by exposing a GetAwaiter method that lets the caller attach a *continuation*:

```
Task<int> task = ComplexCalculationAsync();
var awaiter = task.GetAwaiter();
awaiter.OnCompleted (() =>          // Continuation
{
  int result = awaiter.GetResult();
  Console.WriteLine (result);       // 116
});
```

This says to the operation, "When you finish, execute the specified delegate." Our continuation first calls GetResult, which returns the result of the calculation. (Or, if the task *faulted*—threw an exception—calling GetResult rethrows that exception.) Our continuation then writes out the result via Console.WriteLine.

The await and async Keywords

The await keyword simplifies the attaching of continuations. Starting with a basic scenario, the compiler expands

```
var result = await expression;
statement(s);
```

into something functionally similar to the following:

```
var awaiter = expression.GetAwaiter();
awaiter.OnCompleted (() =>
{
  var result = awaiter.GetResult();
  statement(s);
});
```

NOTE

The compiler also emits code to optimize the scenario of the operation completing synchronously (immediately). A common reason for an asynchronous operation completing immediately is if it implements an internal caching mechanism, and the result is already cached.

Hence, we can call the `ComplexCalculationAsync` method we defined previously, like this:

```
int result = await ComplexCalculationAsync();
Console.WriteLine (result);
```

To compile, we need to add the `async` modifier to the containing method:

```
async void Test()
{
  int result = await ComplexCalculationAsync();
  Console.WriteLine (result);
}
```

The `async` modifier instructs the compiler to treat `await` as a keyword rather than an identifier should an ambiguity arise within that method (this ensures that code written prior to C# 5.0 that might use `await` as an identifier will still compile without error). The `async` modifier can be applied only to methods (and lambda expressions) that return `void` or (as you'll see later) a `Task` or `Task<TResult>`.

NOTE

The `async` modifier is similar to the `unsafe` modifier in that it has no effect on a method's signature or public metadata; it affects only what happens *within* the method.

Methods with the `async` modifier are called *asynchronous functions* because they themselves are typically asynchronous. To see why, let's look at how execution proceeds through an asynchronous function.

Upon encountering an `await` expression, execution (normally) returns to the caller—rather like with `yield return` in an iterator. But before returning, the runtime attaches a continuation to the awaited task, ensuring that when the task completes, execution jumps back into the method and continues where it left off. If the task faults, its exception is rethrown (by virtue of calling GetResult); otherwise, its return value is assigned to the await expression.

NOTE

The CLR's implementation of a task awaiter's OnComple ted method ensures that, by default, continuations are posted through the current *synchronization context*, if one is present. In practice, this means that in rich-client UI scenarios (WPF, UWP, and Windows Forms), if you await on a UI thread, your code will continue on that same thread. This simplifies thread safety.

The expression upon which you await is typically a task; however, any object with a GetAwaiter method that returns an *awaitable object*—implementing INotifyCompletion.OnComple ted and with an appropriately typed GetResult method (and a bool IsCompleted property that tests for synchronous completion)—will satisfy the compiler.

Notice that our await expression evaluates to an int type; this is because the expression that we awaited was a Task<int> (whose GetAwaiter().GetResult() method returns an int).

Awaiting a nongeneric task is legal and generates a void expression:

```
await Task.Delay (5000);
Console.WriteLine ("Five seconds passed!");
```

Task.Delay is a static method that returns a Task that completes in the specified number of milliseconds. The *synchronous* equivalent of Task.Delay is Thread.Sleep.

Task is the nongeneric base class of Task<TResult> and is functionally equivalent to Task<TResult> except that it has no result.

Capturing Local State

The real power of `await` expressions is that they can appear almost anywhere in code. Specifically, an `await` expression can appear in place of any expression (within an asynchronous function) except for within a `catch` or `finally` block, a `lock` expression, or an `unsafe` context.

In the following example, we `await` within a loop:

```
async void Test()
{
  for (int i = 0; i < 10; i++)
  {
    int result = await ComplexCalculationAsync();
    Console.WriteLine (result);
  }
}
```

Upon first executing `ComplexCalculationAsync`, execution returns to the caller by virtue of the `await` expression. When the method completes (or faults), execution resumes where it left off, with the values of local variables and loop counters preserved. The compiler achieves this by translating such code into a state machine, like it does with iterators.

Without the `await` keyword, the manual use of continuations means that you must write something equivalent to a state machine. This is traditionally what makes asynchronous programming difficult.

Writing Asynchronous Functions

With any asynchronous function, you can replace the `void` return type with a `Task` to make the method itself *usefully* asynchronous (and awaitable). No further changes are required:

```
async Task PrintAnswerToLife()
{
  await Task.Delay (5000);
  int answer = 21 * 2;
  Console.WriteLine (answer);
}
```

Notice that we don't explicitly return a task in the method body. The compiler manufactures the task, which it signals upon completion of the method (or upon an unhandled exception). This makes it easy to create asynchronous call chains:

```
async Task Go()
{
  await PrintAnswerToLife();
  Console.WriteLine ("Done");
}
```

(And because Go returns a Task, Go itself is awaitable.) The compiler expands asynchronous functions that return tasks into code that (indirectly) uses TaskCompletionSource to create a task that it then signals or faults.

NOTE

TaskCompletionSource is a CLR type that lets you create tasks that you manually control, signaling them as complete with a result (or as faulted with an exception). Unlike Task.Run, TaskCompletionSource doesn't tie up a thread for the duration of the operation. It's also used for writing I/O-bound task-returning methods (such as Task.Delay).

The aim is to ensure that when a task-returning asynchronous method finishes, execution can jump back to whoever awaited it, via a continuation.

Returning Task<TResult>

You can return a Task<TResult> if the method body returns TResult:

```
async Task<int> GetAnswerToLife()
{
  await Task.Delay (5000);
  int answer = 21 * 2;
  // answer is int so our method returns Task<int>
```

```
    return answer;
  }
```

We can demonstrate `GetAnswerToLife` by calling it from `PrintAnswerToLife` (which is, in turn, called from `Go`):

```
async Task Go()
{
  await PrintAnswerToLife();
  Console.WriteLine ("Done");
}
async Task PrintAnswerToLife()
{
  int answer = await GetAnswerToLife();
  Console.WriteLine (answer);
}
async Task<int> GetAnswerToLife()
{
  await Task.Delay (5000);
  int answer = 21 * 2;
  return answer;
}
```

Asynchronous functions make asynchronous programming similar to synchronous programming. Here's the synchronous equivalent of our call graph, for which calling `Go()` gives the same result after blocking for five seconds:

```
void Go()
{
  PrintAnswerToLife();
  Console.WriteLine ("Done");
}
void PrintAnswerToLife()
{
  int answer = GetAnswerToLife();
  Console.WriteLine (answer);
}
int GetAnswerToLife()
{
  Thread.Sleep (5000);
  int answer = 21 * 2;
  return answer;
}
```

This also illustrates the basic principle of how to design with asynchronous functions in C#, which is to write your methods synchronously, and then replace *synchronous* method calls with *asynchronous* method calls, and `await` them.

Parallelism

We've just demonstrated the most common pattern, which is to `await` task-returning functions immediately after calling them. This results in sequential program flow that's logically similar to the synchronous equivalent.

Calling an asynchronous method without awaiting it allows the code that follows to execute in parallel. For example, the following executes `PrintAnswerToLife` twice, concurrently:

```
var task1 = PrintAnswerToLife();
var task2 = PrintAnswerToLife();
await task1; await task2;
```

By awaiting both operations afterward, we "end" the parallelism at that point (and rethrow any exceptions from those tasks). The `Task` class provides a static method called `WhenAll` to achieve the same result slightly more efficiently. `WhenAll` returns a task that completes when all of the tasks that you pass to it complete:

```
await Task.WhenAll (PrintAnswerToLife(),
                    PrintAnswerToLife());
```

`WhenAll` is called a *task combinator*. (The `Task` class also provides a task combinator called `WhenAny`, which completes when *any* of the tasks provided to it complete.) We cover the task combinators in detail in *C# 8.0 in a Nutshell*.

Asynchronous Lambda Expressions

Just as ordinary *named* methods can be asynchronous

```
async Task NamedMethod()
{
  await Task.Delay (1000);
```

```
  Console.WriteLine ("Foo");
}
```

so, too, can *unnamed* methods (lambda expressions and anonymous methods), if preceded by the async keyword:

```
Func<Task> unnamed = async () =>
{
  await Task.Delay (1000);
  Console.WriteLine ("Foo");
};
```

You can call and await these in the same way:

```
await NamedMethod();
await unnamed();
```

You can use asynchronous lambda expressions when attaching event handlers:

```
myButton.Click += async (sender, args) =>
{
  await Task.Delay (1000);
  myButton.Content = "Done";
};
```

This is more succinct than the following, which has the same effect:

```
myButton.Click += ButtonHandler;
...
async void ButtonHander (object sender, EventArgs args)
{
  await Task.Delay (1000);
  myButton.Content = "Done";
};
```

Asynchronous lambda expressions can also return Task<TResult>:

```
Func<Task<int>> unnamed = async () =>
{
  await Task.Delay (1000);
  return 123;
};
int answer = await unnamed();
```

Asynchronous Streams (C# 8)

C# 8 introduces explicit support for asynchronous enumerators and iterators (*asynchronous streams*). This support builds on the following pair of interfaces, which are asynchronous counterparts to the enumeration interfaces we described in "Enumeration and Iterators" on page 144:

```
public interface IAsyncEnumerable<out T>
{
  IAsyncEnumerator<T> GetAsyncEnumerator (...);
}

public interface IAsyncEnumerator<out T>:
IAsyncDisposable
{
  T Current { get; }
  ValueTask<bool> MoveNextAsync();
}
```

ValueTask<T> is a struct that wraps Task<T>, and is behaviorally equivalent to Task<T>, except that it enables more efficient execution when the task completes synchronously (which can happen often when enumerating a sequence). IAsyncDisposable is an asynchronous version of IDisposable and provides an opportunity to perform cleanup should you choose to manually implement the interfaces:

```
public interface IAsyncDisposable
{
  ValueTask DisposeAsync();
}
```

To generate an asynchronous stream, you write a method that combines the principles of iterators and asynchronous methods. In other words, your method should include both yield return and await, and it should return IAsyncEnumerable<T>:

```
async IAsyncEnumerable<int> RangeAsync (
  int start, int count, int delay)
{
  for (int i = start; i < start + count; i++)
  {
    await Task.Delay (delay);
    yield return i;
  }
}
```

To consume an asynchronous stream, use the await foreach statement:

```
await foreach (var number in RangeAsync (0, 10, 100))
  Console.WriteLine (number);
```

Unsafe Code and Pointers

C# supports direct memory manipulation via pointers within blocks of code marked unsafe and compiled with the /unsafe compiler option. Pointer types are primarily useful for interoperability with C APIs, but you also can use them for accessing memory outside the managed heap or for performance-critical hotspots.

Pointer Basics

For every value type or reference type *V*, there is a corresponding pointer type *V**. A pointer instance holds the address of a variable. Pointer types can be (unsafely) cast to any other pointer type. Following are the main pointer operators:

Operator	Meaning
&	The *address-of* operator returns a pointer to the address of a variable.
*	The *dereference* operator returns the variable at the address of a pointer.
->	The *pointer-to-member* operator is a syntactic shortcut, in which x->y is equivalent to (*x).y.

Unsafe Code

By marking a type, type member, or statement block with the `unsafe` keyword, you're permitted to use pointer types and perform C++-style pointer operations on memory within that scope. Here is an example of using pointers to quickly process a bitmap:

```
unsafe void BlueFilter (int[,] bitmap)
{
  int length = bitmap.Length;
  fixed (int* b = bitmap)
  {
    int* p = b;
    for (int i = 0; i < length; i++)
      *p++ &= 0xFF;
  }
}
```

Unsafe code can run faster than a corresponding safe implementation. In this case, the code would have required a nested loop with array indexing and bounds checking. An unsafe C# method can also be faster than calling an external C function because there is no overhead associated with leaving the managed execution environment.

The fixed Statement

The fixed statement is required to pin a managed object such as the bitmap in the previous example. During the execution of a program, many objects are allocated and deallocated from the heap. To avoid unnecessary waste or fragmentation of memory, the garbage collector moves objects around. Pointing to an object is futile if its address could change while referencing it, so the fixed statement instructs the garbage collector to "pin" the object and not move it around. This can have an impact on the efficiency of the runtime, so you should use fixed blocks only briefly, and you should avoid heap allocation within the fixed block.

Within a fixed statement, you can get a pointer to a value type, an array of value types, or a string. In the case of arrays and strings, the pointer will actually point to the first element, which is a value type.

Value types declared inline within reference types require the reference type to be pinned, as follows:

```
class Test
{
  int x;
  unsafe static void Main()
  {
    Test test = new Test();
    fixed (int* p = &test.x)   // Pins test
    {
      *p = 9;
    }
    System.Console.WriteLine (test.x);
  }
}
```

The Pointer-to-Member Operator

In addition to the & and * operators, C# also provides the C++-style -> operator, which you can use on structs:

```
struct Test
{
  int x;
  unsafe static void Main()
  {
    Test test = new Test();
    Test* p = &test;
    p->x = 9;
    System.Console.WriteLine (test.x);
  }
}
```

The stackalloc Keyword

You can allocate memory in a block on the stack explicitly with the stackalloc keyword. Because it is allocated on the stack, its lifetime is limited to the execution of the method, just as with any other local variable. The block can use the [] operator to index into memory:

```
int* a = stackalloc int [10];
for (int i = 0; i < 10; ++i)
  Console.WriteLine (a[i]);    // Print raw memory
```

Fixed-size buffers

To allocate a block of memory within a struct, use the fixed keyword:

```
unsafe struct UnsafeUnicodeString
{
  public short Length;
  public fixed byte Buffer[30];
}

unsafe class UnsafeClass
{
  UnsafeUnicodeString uus;

  public UnsafeClass (string s)
```

```
    {
      uus.Length = (short)s.Length;
      fixed (byte* p = uus.Buffer)
        for (int i = 0; i < s.Length; i++)
          p[i] = (byte) s[i];
    }
  }
```

Fixed-size buffers are not arrays: If Buffer were an array, it would consist of a reference to an object stored on the (managed) heap, rather than 30 bytes within the struct itself.

The fixed keyword is also used in this example to pin the object on the heap that contains the buffer (which will be the instance of UnsafeClass).

void*

A *void pointer* (void*) makes no assumptions about the type of the underlying data and is useful for functions that deal with raw memory. An implicit conversion exists from any pointer type to void*. A void* cannot be dereferenced, and arithmetic operations cannot be performed on void pointers. For example:

```
unsafe static void Main()
{
  short[] a = {1,1,2,3,5,8,13,21,34,55};
  fixed (short* p = a)
  {
    //sizeof returns size of value-type in bytes
    Zap (p, a.Length * sizeof (short));
  }
  foreach (short x in a)
    System.Console.WriteLine (x);  // Prints all zeros
}

unsafe static void Zap (void* memory, int byteCount)
{
  byte* b = (byte*) memory;
    for (int i = 0; i < byteCount; i++)
      *b++ = 0;
}
```

Preprocessor Directives

Preprocessor directives supply the compiler with additional information about regions of code. The most common preprocessor directives are the conditional directives, which provide a way to include or exclude regions of code from compilation. For example:

```
#define DEBUG
class MyClass
{
  int x;
  void Foo()
  {
    #if DEBUG
    Console.WriteLine ("Testing: x = {0}", x);
    #endif
  }
  ...
}
```

In this class, the statement in Foo is compiled as conditionally dependent upon the presence of the DEBUG symbol. If we remove the DEBUG symbol, the statement is not compiled. Preprocessor symbols can be defined within a source file (as we have done), or passed to the compiler with the /define:*symbol* command-line option, or in the project file if you're using Visual Studio or MSBuild.

With the #if and #elif directives, you can use the ||, &&, and ! operators to perform *or*, *and*, and *not* operations on multiple symbols. The following directive instructs the compiler to include the code that follows if the TESTMODE symbol is defined and the DEBUG symbol is not defined:

```
#if TESTMODE && !DEBUG
  ...
```

Keep in mind, however, that you're not building an ordinary C# expression, and the symbols upon which you operate have absolutely no connection to *variables*—static or otherwise.

The #error and #warning symbols prevent accidental misuse of conditional directives by making the compiler generate a warning or error given an undesirable set of compilation symbols.

Table 14 describes the complete list of preprocessor directives.

Table 14. Preprocessor directives

Preprocessor directive	Action
#define *symbol*	Defines *symbol*.
#undef *symbol*	Undefines *symbol*.
#if *symbol* [*operator symbol2*]...	Conditional compilation (*operator*s are ==, !=, &&, and ||).
#else	Executes code to subsequent #endif.
#elif *symbol* [*operator symbol2*]	Combines #else branch and #if test.
#endif	Ends conditional directives.
#warning *text*	*text* of the warning to appear in compiler output.
#error *text*	*text* of the error to appear in compiler output.
#line [*number* ["*file*"] | hidden]	*number* specifies the line in source code; *file* is the filename to appear in computer output; hidden instructs debuggers to skip over code from this point until the next #line directive.
#region *name*	Marks the beginning of an outline.
#endregion	Ends an outline region.
#pragma warning	See the next section.
#nullable *option*	See "Nullable Reference Types (C# 8)" on page 154.

Pragma Warning

The compiler generates a warning when it spots something in your code that seems unintentional. Unlike errors, warnings don't ordinarily prevent your application from compiling.

Compiler warnings can be extremely valuable in spotting bugs. Their usefulness, however, is undermined when you get *false* warnings. In a large application, maintaining a good signal-to-noise ratio is essential if the "real" warnings are to be noticed.

To this effect, the compiler allows you to selectively suppress warnings with the #pragma warning directive. In this example, we instruct the compiler not to warn us about the field Message not being used:

```
public class Foo
{
  static void Main() { }

  #pragma warning disable 414
  static string Message = "Hello";
  #pragma warning restore 414
}
```

Omitting the number in the #pragma warning directive disables or restores all warning codes.

If you are thorough in applying this directive, you can compile with the /warnaserror switch—this instructs the compiler to treat any residual warnings as errors.

XML Documentation

A *documentation comment* is a piece of embedded XML that documents a type or member. A documentation comment comes immediately before a type or member declaration and starts with three slashes:

```
/// <summary>Cancels a running query.</summary>
public void Cancel() { ... }
```

Multiline comments can be done either like this

```
/// <summary>
/// Cancels a running query
/// </summary>
public void Cancel() { ... }
```

or like this (notice the extra star at the start):

```
/**
    <summary> Cancels a running query. </summary>
*/
public void Cancel() { ... }
```

If you compile with the /doc directive (or enable XML documentation in the project file), the compiler extracts and collates documentation comments into a single XML file. This has two main uses:

- If placed in the same folder as the compiled assembly, Visual Studio automatically reads the XML file and uses the information to provide IntelliSense member listings to consumers of the assembly of the same name.

- Third-party tools (such as Sandcastle and NDoc) can transform the XML file into an HTML help file.

Standard XML Documentation Tags

Here are the standard XML tags that Visual Studio and documentation generators recognize:

`<summary>`

> `<summary>...</summary>`

> Indicates the tool tip that IntelliSense should display for the type or member. Typically, a single phrase or sentence.

`<remarks>`

> `<remarks>...</remarks>`

> Additional text that describes the type or member. Documentation generators pick this up and merge it into the bulk of a type or member's description.

<param>

```
<param name="name">...</param>
```

Explains a parameter on a method.

<returns>

```
<returns>...</returns>
```

Explains the return value for a method.

<exception>

```
<exception [cref="type"]>...</exception>
```

Lists an exception that a method might throw (cref refers to the exception type).

<permission>

```
<permission [cref="type"]>...</permission>
```

Indicates an IPermission type required by the documented type or member.

<example>

```
<example>...</example>
```

Denotes an example (used by documentation generators). This usually contains both description text and source code (source code is typically within a <c> or <code> tag).

<c>

```
<c>...</c>
```

Indicates an inline code snippet. This tag is usually used within an <example> block.

<code>

```
<code>...</code>
```

Indicates a multiline code sample. This tag is usually used within an <example> block.

<see>

```
<see cref="member">...</see>
```

Inserts an inline cross-reference to another type or member. HTML documentation generators typically convert this to a hyperlink. The compiler emits a warning if the type or member name is invalid.

`<seealso>`

```
<seealso cref="member">...</seealso>
```

Cross-references another type or member. Documentation generators typically write this into a separate "See Also" section at the bottom of the page.

`<paramref>`

```
<paramref name="name"/>
```

References a parameter from within a `<summary>` or `<remarks>` tag.

`<list>`

```
<list type=[ bullet | number | table ]>
  <listheader>
    <term>...</term>
    <description>...</description>
  </listheader>
  <item>
    <term>...</term>
    <description>...</description>
  </item>
</list>
```

Instructs documentation generators to emit a bulleted, numbered, or table-style list.

`<para>`

```
<para>...</para>
```

Instructs documentation generators to format the contents into a separate paragraph.

`<include>`

```
<include file='filename' path='tagpath[@name="id"]'>
    ...
</include>
```

Merges an external XML file that contains documentation. The path attribute denotes an XPath query to a specific element in that file.

Index

C

C#

C#
  compiler, 4
  sample program, 2-5
callbacks
  asynchronous functions and, 204
  versus delegates, 118
caller info attributes, 203
capping, accessibility, 99
captured variables, 131
capturing iteration variables, 132
capturing local state, 209
capturing outer variables, 131
carriage return (\r) character, 27
case keyword (see switch statements)
Cast operator, 186
casting (see also boxing)
  as operator, 85
  is operator, 86
  reducing with generics, 108
  upcasting and downcasting, 84
catch blocks, 135
catch clause, 137
changing the flow of execution with braces, 55
char (character) type, 27
checked operator, 22
class constraints, 113
classes
  abstract, 87
  basic program operation, 3
  constants in, 68
  declaring, 67
  deconstructors, 72
  fields in, 67
  finalizers, 80
  indexers, 78
  inheritance (see inheritance)
  instance constructors, 70
  versus interfaces, 100

  methods and, 69
  nameof operator, 82
  object initializers, 73
  object type (see objects)
  partial types and methods, 81
  properties, 75
  sealing, 88
  static classes, 80
  static constructors, 79
  versus structs, 96
  subclassing generic types, 113
  this reference, 74
closures, 131
code examples, obtaining and using, 1
collection initializers, 145
comment notation, 2, 8
common exception types, 143
comparison operators, 25
comparisons, string, 30
compilation
  basics of, 4
  pragma warning, 222
complement (~) operator, 23
composing sequences, 148
compound assignment operators, 46
concatenation (+) operator, 29, 196
conditional and (&&) operator, 26
conditional operators, 26
conditional OR (||) operator, 26
conflicts, avoiding in keywords, 7
const keyword, 68
constants, 8, 68
constraints, 112
constructors
  filed initialization order and, 80
  implicit parameterless, 71
  inheritance and, 89
  instance constructors, 70

About the Authors

Joseph Albahari is the author of the past several editions of *C# 8.0 in a Nutshell* and *C# 8.0 Pocket Reference*, as well as *LINQ Pocket Reference*. He also wrote LINQPad—the popular code scratchpad and LINQ querying utility.

Ben Albahari is cofounder of Auditionist, a casting website for actors in the UK. He was a Program Manager at Microsoft for five years, where he worked on several projects, including the .NET Compact Framework and ADO.NET. He was the cofounder of Genamics, a provider of tools for C# and J++ programmers, as well as software for DNA and protein sequence analysis. He is a coauthor of *C# Essentials*, the first C# book from O'Reilly, and of previous editions of *C# in a Nutshell*.

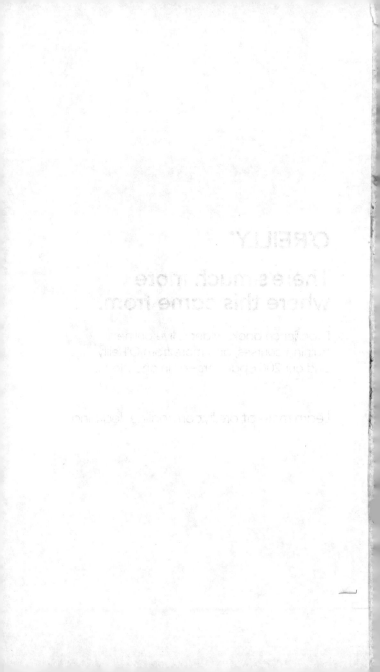